Praise for *Homeschoo...*

A lifestyle of home education is not for th... be difficulties to face and plenty of strugg... ...... way. But we don't have to let the challenges define our lives or our learning—we can face them, conquer them, and continue on our journey. In *Homeschool Bravely*, Jamie Erickson offers us both a beautiful pep talk and a strategic battle plan to keep us moving forward in grace and freedom, discarding perfection and fear as we go.

Jamie C. Martin
Editor of SimpleHomeschool.net and author of *Give Your Child the World*

Homeschooling, like mothering, is *not* a spectator sport. There's never been one perfect way to homeschool and, I'm sure you know, none of us have ever done it perfectly. But from time to time you connect with someone who has authentic insight and profound wisdom into the many facets of homeschooling. In her wonderful, beautifully written new book, *Homeschool Bravely*, Jamie Erickson encourages you to be the homeschool mama He *created* you to be, not the one you *wish* you could be. If God has called you to homeschool, Jamie shows you how to do it with courage . . . even when you're scared out of your wits! Jamie fills each page with down-to-earth, messy stories of faith and failure, self-doubt and self-care, taking your hand and walking with you, sharing how she's learned to stay calm in the chaos and how she's found the balance between striving for perfection and learning it's not all up to you. As Jamie so beautifully illustrates, God is with you on your homeschooling journey, *and He has all the answers you'll ever need*. Oh, how I wish I'd had Jamie's book when I was homeschooling! With practical tips and ideas, Jamie will give you the courage to help you navigate the chaotic world of homeschooling with divine, remarkable grace! Let her take your hand and walk with you on your homeschool journey.

Kate Battistelli
Author of *Growing Great Kids* and *The God Dare*; former homeschooling mom to her daughter, GRAMMY award-winning artist, Francesca Battistelli

Jamie Erickson's been reading your mail, and you'll be glad she did! Even though I am a retired homeschool momma, I couldn't put her book down. With humor, empathy, and biblical wisdom, Jamie names our fears and calls us to stand bravely—putting our confidence in Him, not ourselves. While packed full of practical suggestions, *Homeschool Bravely* at its heart provides a solidly biblical framework for homeschooling with faith in His promises. If you believe God's called you to homeschooling, this is the book to keep on your nightstand.

Debra Bell
Author of *The Ultimate Guide to Homeschooling*

Authentic, witty, and relatable, Jamie offers hope for the fearful homeschooling mother. She shows us all how to walk in freedom and not fear. She's packed this entire book with raw and candid peeks into her real-life homeschool, has shared practical tips for dealing with the everyday struggles, and has generously pointed everything back to the God who can handle every fault and failure. *Homeschool Bravely* is the push that we all need to stay the course with courage.

Pam Barnhill
Author of *Better Together* and host of the *Homeschool Solutions Show* podcast

For the Christian mother who's just about at the end of her homeschool rope: this book could be the healing balm your soul needs. Jamie is refreshingly real, relentlessly encouraging, and full of Scripture. My most favorite parts, though, were the practical ones. *Homeschool Bravely* is brimming with fresh, doable ideas to transform bad days, occupy toddlers, and refresh your mama soul!

Jessica Smartt
Author of *Memory-Making Mom: Building Traditions That Breathe Life into Your Home*

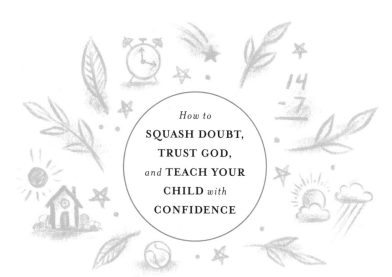

How to
SQUASH DOUBT,
TRUST GOD,
and **TEACH YOUR**
CHILD *with*
CONFIDENCE

HOMESCHOOL
Bravely

Jamie Erickson

MOODY PUBLISHERS

CHICAGO

Published in association with the literary agency of WordServe Literary Group, www.wordserverliterary.com.

Edited by Annette LaPlaca
Interior design: Erik M. Peterson
Cover design and illustrations by Connie Gabbert
Author photo: Dain Erickson

Library of Congress Cataloging-in-Publication Data

Names: Erickson, Jamie (Homeschool teacher), author.
Title: Homeschool bravely : how to squash doubt, trust God, and teach your child with confidence / Jamie Erickson.
Other titles: Home school bravely
Description: Chicago : Moody Publishers, [2019] | Includes bibliographical references.
Identifiers: LCCN 2018061483 (print) | LCCN 2019010419 (ebook) | ISBN 9780802497598 (ebook) | ISBN 9780802418876
Subjects: LCSH: Home schooling--United States--Handbooks, manuals, etc. | Christian education--United States--Handbooks, manuals, etc.
Classification: LCC LC40 (ebook) | LCC LC40 .E75 2019 (print) | DDC 371.04/20973--dc23
LC record available at https://lccn.loc.gov/2018061483

ISBN: 978-0-8024-1887-6

To Maddie, Reese, Finn, Jack, and Jude.
Teachers aren't supposed to have favorite students.
You will always be mine.

Contents

PART 1
The Fear

Fear will be a threat whenever you set out to pursue
a desire that means something to you.

EMILY P. FREEMAN
A Million Little Ways

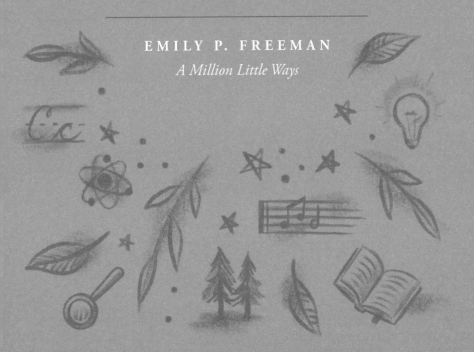

I

When You Check the Wrong Box

In the next few years, I'd like to see you transition her to public school. Kudos to you for homeschooling during those early years, but she's in seventh grade now and needs to have some experience in a *real* school," she said, punctuating the word *real* with an empathetic smile toward my daughter. "We're finding that homeschooled kids just don't transition to college well. In fact, most colleges refuse to enroll them. You understand, don't you? It's for her own good."

For her own good.

With those four little words, all my anxiety—all the fears of failure that I thought I had packaged up and tucked away years ago—began to resurface. As the doctor stared at me in her crisp white lab coat surrounded by several neatly framed diplomas all touting golden seals of approval, I could feel the tension begin to build, twisting my stomach into knots as hot tears of disappointment filled my eyes, threatening to fall unbidden down my cheeks.

I began to scramble for any scrap of courage—any words of response I could muster. But nothing came. I just sat there, beaten by her hidden accusations and verbal professional punches.

I had brought my daughter, Maddie, into the clinic that morning for her annual check-up. Now in seventh grade, she was at an age when seeing her male pediatrician, whom we had known and loved for years, was beginning to make her feel slightly awkward. In a desperate attempt to help her feel confident in talking about all the big body changes on the horizon, I decided to take her to a female doctor. I had asked around for recommendations of potential physicians from friends, but none were given. So in a fine moment of mothering, I eenie-meenie-minie-moed my way through the phone book and landed on a doctor's name that sounded promising, as if one can tell anything about a person from her last name. It seemed like a good idea at the time.

What started as an appointment meant to help my daughter feel brave about her body ended up leaving me in fear. What was supposed to be half an hour of physical examination turned into thirty minutes of emotional and social assessment. The doctor held Maddie's new patient forms in hand, casually glanced at the pages of health history, and began tapping her pen on the clipboard in a methodical rhythm. Her eyes were fixed. Her brow was furrowed. I followed her gaze down to the stack of papers—a black and white resume of the past twelve years of my daughter's life written in my own hand. She seemed to be focused on one particular question on the form: *Does your child currently attend school? If so, please check the box indicating whether the school is public, private, or other.*

Naturally, I had checked *other.*

"Does she have any friends—any peers that she can confide in?" the doctor questioned. "What is your plan in the coming years to transition her to normal life? Homeschooling was fine for those early days, but don't you think she needs to begin learning how to function independently from you? She's almost in high school, after all."

Poor Maddie tucked her hands under her legs and scrunched down deep in her chair, desperate to somehow disappear beneath its cold vinyl. She looked so small and a little embarrassed, sitting in awkward silence, trapped between opposing viewpoints. Before I could offer my daughter a few reassuring words, the doctor clucked her tongue in obvious disapproval and continued with her questions. It was an inquisition—a battle—and I was on the losing side. I had clearly checked the "wrong" box. I internally curled myself up into a protective shell, a mental paralysis, and could not seem to form any kind of verbal response or defense.

Even though as a certified, trained teacher I had spent years in a traditional school teaching other people's children how to be "normal" (whatever that means), even though I had launched and led a monthly homeschool mothers' group in the past, even though I had contributed to not one but three books on homeschooling well, and even though I made my living writing a blog dedicated to encouraging and equipping homeschool mothers, I left the doctor's office that day feeling inadequate. That wasn't the first time fear weaseled its way into my mother-heart, and it would certainly not be the last.

> I left the doctor's office that day feeling inadequate. That wasn't the first time fear weaseled its way into my mother-heart, and it would certainly not be the last.

Most mothers, myself included, live in a committed, lifelong relationship with self-doubt. Fear, anxiety, and tension seem always to be the by-products of our love and investment. We hear the gentle whispers of worry and wonder if we can raise our children right, raise them well, raise them at all. For the homeschool mother, that self-doubt is magnified by the full weight of her child's education. She feels the burden of proof: that her children will learn all they need to know and be as good if not better than those being taught by the other guys. And if they don't? Well, the blame must surely fall to her. She spends her days in mental and emotional apathy, convinced that she's somehow going to ruin her kids.

Over the last five years since I began *The Unlikely Homeschool* blog, I've received thousands of messages from mothers secretly suffocating in fear, all questioning their decision to combine home and school. These are the kinds of anxiety-filled ramblings I've heard again and again (perhaps you've rehearsed a few of them yourself):

- "The public schools have billions of dollars at their disposal to educate the masses. I can barely afford any curriculum, let alone, the right one."

- "Would switching curriculums help my struggling learner? And if I switch, what if I leave learning gaps? What if I don't cover all that needs to be covered? What if I miss something?"

- "What about my strong-willed child? My special-needs child? My just-like-me child? I don't know if I can spend another waking minute teaching my difficult one."

- "Perhaps I'm failing because I'm not organized enough. Patient enough. Creative enough. Maybe I'm just not enough."

- "What if my kids end up blaming me for my decision to keep them at home?"

- "In the busyness of the homeschool day, I feel like I'm completely neglecting my baby, my toddler, and even myself. How can I continue being a mother and a teacher without losing my mind?"

- "The day-in and day-out is so monotonous. My kids don't ever seem to get along. I spend most of my days settling one sibling squabble after another. I thought homeschooling was supposed to build family bonds."

- "My extended family has never been on board. I'm tired of facing the firing squad at every holiday and family get-together. How can I convince them that my choice to homeschool was the right one if I'm not so sure myself?"

Perhaps you feel like someone else could do a better job teaching your kids than you can. Maybe you see the lack of letters behind your name as concrete proof that you are unqualified to teach and that it's no wonder your eight-year-old still can't read at grade level. It's possible you're panicking over the social well-being of your child—you don't know any other homeschoolers and don't want your kids to continue in isolation. Perhaps you are tapped out, emotionally and physically drained from years of just slogging through. You're tired of having to play the Enforcer when your teenager refuses to do his work each day. Home-schooling has not lived up to your expectations, and you're wondering if spinning all these plates is even worth it—wondering if you made the wrong choice. Collectively, these concerns combine to make an unhealthy and unhelpful personal narrative all too common for those of us who have chosen the path less taken.

You see, when you stepped through door number three and checked the "other" box, you opted to swim upstream, joining a group of people who have decided to go in a different edu-cational direction from the rest of the world. And different is always a little bit scary, especially as it relates to your kids.

The "normal" school down the street has decades of gradu-ates with which to validate their way of educating. And while homeschooling has reached second-generation status, it boasts a far fewer number of graduates. It's not as easy to confirm the success of the *different* way because its verdict is still out. It seems more natural to trust the public (or private) school treadmill because it has formulas, experts, and billions of dollars at its dis-posal. As a mom, you have no twelve-step plans, no formulas for success; and you certainly don't have a billion-dollar budget. So how can you ever hope to educate your kids *the right way*? (As if there even is a one-size-fits-all *right way* to teach that works for every child.)

It would be so much easier if homeschooling came with a just-add-water-and-stir tag, but it doesn't. It comes with a lot of questions. It comes with a lot of unknowns. Consequently, it often comes with a lot of fears. If left unchecked, those fears can begin to suffocate and rob you of the many gifts of homeschooling that were the very reasons you chose this unconventional path in the first place.

It's time to end the fear. It's time to stand tall and be brave.

> Left unchecked, fears can begin to suffocate and rob you of the many gifts of homeschooling that were the very reasons you chose this unconventional path in the first place.

Since you've picked up this book amidst a sea of homeschooling how-to books, I can only imagine the word *bravely* caught your attention because brave is the very opposite of how you are feeling right now. Maybe you're only a few months in, have hit a hurdle, and are wondering if you've made the wrong choice. Perhaps you've already begun looking for the nearest exit ramp. Maybe you've been homeschooling for a while, you're trapped somewhere in the messy middle, and you're beginning to doubt whether you can continue plodding along. You're not alone. In fact, without support, more than a third of homeschool moms quit within the first year.[1] Something tells me you don't want to join those ranks, however. You're fearful, but you're also in search of help.

For whatever reason, the weight of fear has pulled you toward these pages. But that kind of neurosis is too heavy to hold. To be honest, it wasn't yours to carry in the first place. What you need is anxiety-free homeschooling. What you need is a refocused vision for the story God has uniquely written for you and yours—a homeschooling manifesto. What you need is the courage to check the "wrong" box with bravery.

The normal path to courageous homeschooling is a never-ending, winding journey that will eventually lead to brave. But like most of life's worthwhile adventures, it's usually a two steps forward, one step back sort of shuffle. I don't tell you that to discourage you or make you throw in the towel. I'm only attempting to be transparent and honest with you so that you don't see your fear as a personal failure or a lack of commitment, but instead as a natural part of your progression—one of the many necessary steps you'll take in order to go from where you are now on the journey to where you want to be in the end.

That day in the doctor's office, my fear came marching in, hoping to fill in all the spaces of my heart. I sat there with quotations, statistics, and proofs that homeschooling not only works, but that it works better; and yet I couldn't seem to formulate one word of rebuttal to the doctor's misguided accusations. Not one. When the visit was done, I gathered my daughter and what little self-respect I had left, squared my shoulders in feigned resolve, and walked out feeling anything but brave.

"It's for her own good," replayed in a permanent loop in my head on the drive home. I just couldn't seem to shake it. *Am I really failing her? Have I ruined Maddie and any chance she might have at success in college? On the job? In relationships? Have I been checking the wrong box all along?* These needless and irrational thoughts began swimming around in my brain as they had done so often in the past. I glanced up in the rearview mirror, but when I did, I didn't see the mother who had been teaching her daughter since the very beginning. I didn't see the many countless hours I had spent planning and preparing each and every year. All I saw was *lesser than*. I saw *ill-equipped* and *unable*.

I nearly caved to all my insecurities and misgivings about my abilities to homeschool. Then one verse in Philippians snapped me back to my senses—reminded me of what I already knew. "And I am sure of this, that he who began a good work in you will bring it to completion at the day of Jesus Christ" (Phil. 1:6).

It was *He* who began this work in my daughter, *He* who had

Increasingly high profile universities are actively recruiting homeschooling graduates because they recognize traits they believe will make successful students—highly motivated, self-starters, determined, and with a strong, supportive family backing.[2]
JAMIE C. MARTIN
author of *Give Your Child the World: Raising Globally Minded Kids One Book at a Time*

called me to homeschool, *He* who ordered her days from the very beginning, and *He* who would see it through to completion. It was God who placed the call on my heart when I began feeling a tug toward home education. He later affirmed that call through His Word, through the specific life circumstances He had given me, and through the wisdom and counsel of many other Christians He had placed around me. I was just following in obedience. In my own might, I would fail her; that's true. I'm only human, after all. But He would never fail her. He would always have a better view of "her own good" than I ever could, than that doctor ever could, than every college board ever could.

I began replaying those words from Philippians over and over again in my head, replacing the doctor's indictment, until my heart settled on the Truth and I became brave once again. I hadn't checked the wrong box! If you're homeschooling, neither have you.

I invite you to join me on this path to bravery. I hold out my hand to you, not as one who has planted a victory flag on the top of Mt. Brave, but as a fellow traveler who still has to daily fix her eyes on Jesus for the courage to obey. My bravery is a work in progress. That notorious day at the doctor's proved nothing if not *that*. But, after many years of doing the fearful shuffle—two steps forward, one step back—I've learned a few things about checking the "wrong" box with bravery.

2

Calling or Coincidence

There are two kinds of women in this world: those who wake up in the morning completely unshaken by the choices of the past or the future—women content to live an accidental life—and then all the rest of us.

If you are one of the three women on the planet who lands in the first group, a woman who feels perfectly comfortable living on whim and fancy, going wherever the wind blows with little to no regrets, feel free to give this section a polite golf clap for good effort and skip to chapter three. But if you're like me, habitually hesitant and desperate to have everything about your life clearly defined in outline form, double-spaced with footnotes, then you've probably opened this book looking for neatly packaged childhoods and cinched-up futures for your kids. You're hoping these pages will be like some Magic 8-Ball you can just shake up and find firm direction and confirmation about your home-school. All the many unknowns about teaching your children have left you feeling unsure, perhaps even calloused and bruised. You're beginning to wonder if you made the wrong choice—if the public school could do it better. You don't want to ruin your kids, and you're a bit overwhelmed by the *What Ifs*.

You weren't expecting the way to be so windy or so lonely.

Your life looks nothing like the pretty photo on the cover of the curriculum catalog, which surely must mean you're doing something wrong, right? Apathy has set up camp in your heart, and you just don't want to soldier on anymore. I can understand that. I've been there. To be honest, sometimes I'm still there. While I *love* homeschooling, I don't always *like* it. The days are long, the work is thankless, and for the most part, the physical and mental investment is way above my pay grade, or at least that's the yarn I'm tempted to spin on the hard days.

> While I *love* homeschooling, I don't always *like* it.

When things get bumpy, I start to rehearse my "I quit" speech. I inventory the reasons why homeschooling is a dead-end street: my son still doesn't punctuate his sentences, and I'm starting to think he never will; my high schooler wants to learn chemistry, but the only chemistry I can remember is the kind my husband and I felt on our first date; my house looks like a set from *Hoarders*; and I've been so busy nurturing chaos lately that I'm not really sure when I've washed my hair last. I fixate on all the trouble spots and begin to doubt my decision to homeschool.

On the hard days, I look with longing out the window. I watch as the big yellow bus makes its way down my street, snatching up rambunctious kids and leaving quiet spaces in their place. I sit transfixed, if only for a second, and wonder what it must be like for the moms left waving from the sidewalk. *Do those moms have clean houses? Do those moms get drilled about schooling choice in the grocery store checkout line? Do those moms carry the full weight of their child's education on their shoulders?*

Difficult days will do that to you. They'll leave you wondering and longing for an eject button. And while I would like to say that chaotic homeschooling days are few and far between, you and I both know they are not. I-need-a-do-over days will always be inevitable when combining an imperfect mother with imperfect children in an imperfect world. Fractured people don't always fuse well even when covered over and under with love.

When It Feels Like a Big Fat Coincidence

But might I suggest that the real challenge to homeschooling bravely isn't the homeschooling—the curriculum, the never-ending to-do lists, or the imperfect people? The real challenge is finding your vision and passion for it and then firmly grabbing hold of that vision so the shaky days don't break you. The real challenge is recognizing that homeschooling is a call from God and then fully embracing His call to do it.

But God didn't call me, you might be thinking. *I'm only homeschooling because when I started, it was the most convenient choice for my family.*

Fair enough. For now, we'll go with that answer: You chose your schooling path based on your family dynamics, your finances, your time, your child's needs. God's still, small voice had nothing to do with your decision, so therefore homeschooling is not your *calling*. It's just a big fat coincidence that your particular situation fits nicely with home education.

> The real challenge is finding your vision and passion and then firmly grabbing hold so the shaky days don't break you.

If that's the case, then you're in good company. I've talked with many moms who are homeschooling for similar reasons. Their husbands travel a lot for work, have seasonal jobs or odd schedules. Homeschooling allows their children to maintain thriving relationships with the working parent. Some have a blended family or are caring for aging parents or foster kids, and homeschooling grants them more flexibility. Still others have special-needs kids and need the Individual Education Plans (IEP) that homeschooling permits. They figured schooling at home would allow their children to grow into the very best versions of themselves. I've even heard of moms who chose to homeschool simply because they had a house full of night owls. They had tortured visions of dragging their sleepy-eyed children out of bed, shoving zipper bags of milk-less cereal into their hands, and pushing them out the front door to catch a bus at too-early o'clock in the morning. Homeschooling offered them a gentler alternative.

While all of those reasons might be true in their homes and in yours, as a Christian, I'm inclined to believe there's more to the story than mere happenstance situations or coincidence. It might feel like you backed into this thing by accident or came in through an unmarked side door, but that's simply not true. If you're homeschooling right now, it is because God ordained it for this time. And, dare I say it, He called you to it. Granted, He may not have used a neon sign or writing in the sky, but He called you just the same.

Admittedly, a neon sign, a booming voice from heaven, and even a Gideon-like wet fleece would have been a more obvious directional arrow to the path God prepared for you. But that's only because, in our humanness, you and I don't always

As with any unconventional choice, homeschooling bravely means confidently going forward with what we are certain God has called us to do. Our courage comes from the knowledge that He equips those He calls.[1]
KENDRA FLETCHER
author of *Lost and Found: Losing Religion, Finding Grace*

see Christ standing right there in the midst of our everyday life. Like the men on the road to Emmaus, we don't always recognize Jesus kicking up dirt on the trail right beside us, leading us with the simple situations He's ordained in the monotony of life. But it's Him. He is there.

Your circumstances are where the spirituality and the practicality of God's will converge. You can't always fleece your way to God's calling. You can only deal with what you've been handed. But the comforting truth is that the hand that gave each of these circumstances to you has a purpose and a point for all of them. That's providence. That's *calling*.

Thirty or so years ago when my in-laws decided to homeschool, they didn't hear some audible voice from heaven pushing them in that direction. They didn't read a Bible verse drawing them to one schooling choice over the other. They didn't even ask around for public opinion because the truth is, homeschooling was unheard of back then. The idea of doing school at home sounded ludicrous, even to them. No, they didn't choose homeschooling. God chose it for them. He used real-life circumstances to shove them to this road less traveled.

My husband injured his hip bone. At the age of six, he fell off the kitchen counter and right into a three-year stint of doctor visits, surgeries, and body casts. Hearing of his temporary paralysis, the school system sent a tutor to his bedside each day that first year. By year two, his parents began to see how much he thrived with the one-on-one educational attention. As year two gave way to year three, they began to prayerfully consider the idea of just keeping him at home permanently. Their fleece was a wicked, eight-inch scar on my husband's left thigh that still looks like it came right out of the costume department of a slasher movie. (Stitching straight seams was clearly not the highest priority for surgeons in the mid-80s.) My husband never returned to school after third grade, and his younger brother never even went until his final years of high school.

A broken hip. God used a tangible circumstance to draw my in-laws to homeschool their children. Did they hear God's still, small voice? Did they see Jesus stepping along beside them? No. But He was there, just the same. He orchestrated their specific circumstances so homeschooling became the clear choice. And whether you realize it or not, if you are homeschooling because of your "circumstances," He's done the same for you. You have to open your eyes and look around to see it. In doing so, you just might easily trip over what God placed right in front of you.

> Most likely, God's calling for your life and the life of your kids began with the practical, everyday circumstances He dealt you.

God probably didn't give you writing in the sky, that's true. But let's be honest, He rarely does. Most likely, His calling for your life and the life of your kids began with the practical, everyday circumstances He dealt you. So while your call to homeschool might not have come through an audible voice, if it was whispered in His Providence, it's a calling just the same.

You have to grab hold of that fact before you can go one more step in your quest to find homeschool bravery. Half-in commitments won't hold. Your foundation for homeschooling has to be anchored in God's calling, or like the foolish man who built his house upon the sand, you'll watch your homeschool crumble at the first sign of a storm.

An Act of Worship

Right now, the grass might seem more lush on the other side of the schooling fence. But it's not; it's just different. We'll dive deeper into all of that *different* in Part 2. But for now, let's start seeing homeschooling for what it really is: a chance to trust God. As I look at what appears to be greener grass over there on the school playground, I can easily become preoccupied with comparison and make the calling an idol. But homeschooling is not my god. It's just the work He's given me to do. And the work, when done faithfully, will always lead to worship. When I set aside *my* wants, *my* plans, *my* goals and joyfully embrace the calling God has placed in my life to train my children in this short season, I am offering up worshipful praise to my King. John puts it this way: "When you bear (produce) much fruit, My Father is honored and glorified" (John 15:8 AMPC).

Admittedly, homeschooling doesn't always feel worshipful. But, if my days are "determined" as Job 14 says, then every part of my life, even the mundane bits, have purpose and point. The daily grind of homeschooling and mothering is really holy ground. That diaper that needs to be changed *again*? It's holy ground. That clean load of laundry that's sitting at the foot of my bed waiting to be folded? That's holy ground too. The matchbox car I have to fish out of the toilet bowl is holy ground. Every tiny act of faithfulness I give is a chance to show my love for God through my obedience. It is my chance to daily wash the feet of those around me and to work "as working for the Lord" (Col. 3:23 NIV).

> The daily grind of homeschooling and mothering is really holy ground.

Obeying on the difficult days can sometimes feel like drudgery. But obedience in all things is our one true demonstration of love to God. He said, "I love you," through the blood of His Son. And our faithful obedience is our open-armed "Ditto" (John 14:15). With each step of faith, especially in the hard things, we are composing a chorus of praise. The psalmist wrote, "Just tell me what to do and I will do it, Lord. As long as

I live I'll wholeheartedly obey" (Ps. 119:33–34 TLB). That same ardent worship rang out on the lips of Christ when He said, "Not my will, but yours, be done" (Luke 22:42).

I'll admit, it's easy to forget the still, small voice of the Savior when it's being drowned out by sibling arguments, the tears of frustrated learners, and the awkward plunking of piano keys during music practice. And let's not forget our own inner monologue of negativity. Trouble will always brew when you allow your own narrative to speak louder than the whispers of God. But His voice is always there.

The first part of Psalm 46:10 offers up a great call to action to help us with our noise problem. It says, "Be still, and know that I am God." In our movement toward bravery, we must first be still. While that seems like an oxymoron, it's not. There's a reason Scripture calls us to just *be*. The *knowing* won't ever come without the stillness, without our silence. As a recovering *do* addict, I've always struggled to just *be*. Since you're a mom, you can probably say the same thing. But, if we are to find God's will for our homeschool and be anchored in His calling, we have to quiet our souls. The silence will allow us to hear the Spirit's providential call on those days when we've forgotten it.

A Word of *Rhema*

Fortunately, hearing God's voice in the big things, such as a child's education, requires no more faith than it takes to find His voice in the everyday. He's not clutching it tightly just waiting to see if you can muster up enough strength and tenacity to peel it from his steely grasp. He's holding it out for you. He's inviting you to trust Him with it. Ambiguity is not in His nature. His plans are certain. His way is sure—especially for you, especially in this.

You can pour out lengthy prayers and attempt to sweet-talk God into giving you one sneak peek around the next bend, but you don't need to. His revelation is set and spilled out on every page of Scripture. It's stamped in capital letters for you to claim whenever you need it.

Every summer, as I pack away all-things-last-year and bring out the shiny and new of next fall, I begin to pray. I ask God to give me a specific verse to clutch close for the coming school year. Since I've been around this fear-filled block a time or two thousand, I know that there will come a day in the next nine months when I'll forget His call—when I'll grow weary in my well-doing. My self-proclaimed personal failures will grow seeds of guilt and bitterness and I'll find myself homeschooling out of obligation instead of praise. In His faithfulness, He always answers my prayers and directs me to the exact verses I'll need even before I ever need them.

His Word is timely like that. It's living and active. It's *rhema*. *Rhema* is a funny word. It certainly takes spell-check for a wild ride. It's a Greek noun that makes a human attempt to translate God-breathed words into black-and-white ink. It's first unveiled in Matthew 4:4, "It is written, 'Man shall not live by bread alone, but by every word [*rhema*] that comes from the mouth of God.'" *Rhema* is the life in the Word of God that makes it applicable right here in this very moment for this specific situation. It is where the efficient begins to get intimate. It's where the gospel that covers everyone seeps into the individual souls of humanity. How can the same words spoken throughout the ages woo us all so differently and yet draw us all to the same last page? Because they are *rhema*.

Don't bother scanning your concordance for Truth about *homeschooling*. You won't find that word anywhere in Scripture. But while the Bible might be void of that particular term, it's not mute about education and training. In their book, *Educating the WholeHearted Child*, Clay and Sally Clarkson give us a glimpse at God's opinion of learning in the home: "There are only three divinely established institutions—family, government, and the church. . . . It doesn't make sense to try to impose elements of an institution of man, such as public school, upon an institution of God."[2]

Homeschooling is not for every family. I'd venture to say that it's not even for every Christian family. But I know it's for my family, at least until He shows us a different plan. God uses His *rhema* words each summer to remind me. On the really hard days when I feel I've lost my footing, I can peel back the layers of the verses He's given me and recalibrate my direction.

Here's a peek at some of the *rhema* I've received from Him over the years, as well as a look at the thoughts that have raced through my mind as I've weighed each one of these verses against my own homeschool. No doubt my calling will seem legalistic to some, but please know my heart. I don't believe for a second that homeschooling is the *only* way, that it's *forever* or for a*lways*, or that these verses will be the Scriptural silver-bullet answers to all your fears. (Propping *any* form of education on a spiritual platform, declaring it to be a theological dogma and not just a Christian liberty would be playing fast-and-loose with the Bible.) I only hold these passages out to you as an example of how God has used His Word to show me the way *I* should go.

The first year, God led me to Deuteronomy 11:19: "You shall teach them to your children, talking of them when you are sitting in your house, and when you are walking by the way, and when you lie down, and when you rise." After reading that verse, I realized that, one way or another, my children will be taught by someone at all times, no matter where they are or what they are doing. They will always be watching and will parrot back the words they hear and the actions they see. As the old saying goes, "More is caught than taught." That verse and its *rhema* forced me to ask myself some tough questions: What will my kids be taught at public school? What will my children catch from those around them?

God gave me James 1:27 to guide me to the answers and to help me see homeschooling as one of many tools I can use to

help keep my children from being corrupted by worldly thinking and Godless lifestyles: "Religion that God our Father accepts
as pure and faultless is this: to look after orphans and widows
in their distress and to keep oneself from being polluted by the
world" (NIV).

Some would argue that Christians are not to avoid the world
but to be the "salt and light" in it. I am confident and hopeful
that all of my children will live out the gospel to those around
them, or at least my kids who have accepted Christ's ultimate
sacrifice for their sins (Matt. 5:13–16). God doesn't gift children
with a mini version of the Holy Spirit upon salvation, after all.
The same power that is at work within me as an adult is at work
within them. Even so, God gave me 1 Corinthians 15:33 to remind me that my children's developing years need protection
and guidance: "Do not be deceived: 'Bad company ruins good
morals.'" Slowly but surely, I can disciple my children toward
discipling others, but it feels unlikely that my five-year-old (who
may or may not even have a saving knowledge of Jesus) or my
nine-year-old (who has just begun to grow spiritually) is going
to turn the tide of a spiritually depraved environment. My children have to learn to be faithful in *little* before I can expect their
faithfulness in *much* (Luke 16:10).

Not long after I read the passage in 1 Corinthians, God di-
rected me to 1 Timothy 5:8. It reiterated that responsibility and
placed the primary burden on the shoulders of my husband and
me: "But if anyone does not provide for his relatives, and especially for members of his household, he has denied the faith and is
worse than an unbeliever." As a parent, I'm the provider for those
in my household—for physical needs and spiritual ones. The salvation and sanctification of my children should mean more to me
than anything else. While my children may be influenced by adult
mentors, Sunday school teachers, and youth leaders, my husband and I are to be their chief disciplers. Homeschooling offers
me a unique and increased opportunity to provide for them.

Matthew 19:14 confirmed my choice to help my children draw near to God first before I sent them "into all the world." It reads, "But Jesus said, 'Let the little children come to me and do not hinder them, for to such belongs the kingdom of heaven.'" Whenever Jesus addressed children in Scripture, He always invited them to "come," to gather close to Him, implying a need for protection. His command to "Go and make disciples of all nations" (Matt. 28:19–20 NIV) was not given to little children, but rather, to people who had spent three years under His divine discipleship. He wasn't speaking to children. In fact, every reference in Scripture that relates to raising kids refers to them as immature and in need of nurture and safekeeping. These verses helped me to embrace childhood as a season of preparation.

Later, God reaffirmed my desire to focus my attention on training my children with Luke 6:40: "A disciple is not above his teacher, but everyone when he is fully trained will be like his teacher." Kids need to be discipled by a good teacher before they themselves can become teachers. I cannot expect my first grader to be an influencer in the world at the public school or anywhere else until he is fully trained.

Homeschooling has given my children the chance to walk with firm feet. They've been able to avoid many potential land mines because I've had the freedom to clear the way. Luke 17:1–2 describes the importance of this type of protection during the early years: "Jesus said to his disciples: 'Things that cause people to stumble are bound to come, but woe to anyone through whom they come. It would be better for them to be thrown into the sea with a millstone around their neck than to cause one of these little ones to stumble'" (NIV). Kids can survive and even thrive in public schools, but they can also encounter influences that can cause them to stumble. One day I will answer for the decisions I have made in the training of my children. I hold that weighty *rhema* closely.

When I came across Proverbs 1:7–9, I found that it restated the need for parental instruction and also provided a gentle roadmap toward wisdom: "The fear of the Lord is the beginning of knowledge; fools despise wisdom and instruction. Hear, my son, your father's instruction, and forsake not your mother's teaching, for they are a graceful garland for your head and pendants for your neck."

One summer due to a misaligned focus and an over-packed schedule, I felt irritated and inflamed every time I thought about starting the homeschool year. Even before I had a chance to consider any other schooling option, God pulled my vision to Matthew 12:30: "Whoever is not with me is against me, and whoever does not gather with me scatters." He reinforced what I already knew: all too soon, my kids will leave my home and be inundated with a culture that is directly opposed to God. They'll be fed lies by firehose each and every day. Their only hope is found in the Truth of God's Word. Belief is often a by-product of knowledge. Sunday school stories, while good, are only the tip of the iceberg. Homeschooling offers me the latitude and license to teach my kids solid, biblical literacy. The time I invest now, at home, will help fortify their faith before it is forged in a fire of persecution.

Another time, I had doubts about whether or not my children would be able to cultivate friendships while homeschooling. I formulated quite a fiery monologue of fear in my head.

Proverbs 13:20 quickly extinguished my fright: "Whoever walks with the wise becomes wise, but the companion of fools will suffer harm." The "companions" of a traditional classroom don't always choose to walk wisely. Can I really expect a pack of immature seven-year-olds to be the social and moral compass of my seven-year-old for the majority of each day? The socializing offered through homeschooling, on the other hand, allows my kids to be around many wise people of all ages.

The *rhema* of 1 Timothy 6:20 confirmed my desire to give my children excellence and truth in their education: "Timothy, guard what has been entrusted to your care. Turn away from godless chatter and the opposing ideas of what is falsely called knowledge" (NIV). Government restrictions that prevent teachers from using God's Word in the classroom seem to open the doors to "godless chatter" and "false knowledge." School children are sometimes exposed to teaching that goes way beyond reading, writing, and arithmetic. At times that teaching can be spiritually hostile. Homeschooling, on the other hand, allows me to guard my good deposit, my children.

Philippians 4:8 took the directive to "guard" one step further and actually gave me a blueprint for how to do it: "Finally, brothers, whatever is true, whatever is honorable, whatever is just, whatever is pure, whatever is lovely, whatever is commendable, if there is any excellence, if there is anything worthy of praise, think about these things." Because of homeschooling, I can handpick a curriculum that is true, honorable, just, pure, lovely, and commendable—the things I want my children to think on all day long.

Like the passage from Philippians, 2 Timothy 3:14–15 was another permission slip to focus on the Word of God: "But as for you, continue in what you have learned and have firmly believed, knowing from whom you learned it and how from childhood you have been acquainted with the sacred writings, which are able to make you wise for salvation through faith in Christ Jesus." The emphasis here is placed on learning and being acquainted with Scripture as a child and then continuing on in that knowledge for the rest of one's life. Homeschooling allows me long hours to weave God's Truth into everything my children are learning and to use it as a tool to help them grow a biblical worldview.

Lately God has been drawing me to Proverbs 2:6. It encourages me not only to embrace this opportunity that I've been given to center my children's education on Truth, but also to celebrate it: "For the Lord gives wisdom; from his mouth come knowledge and understanding." Even on the hard days I can see homeschooling as a privilege because I've witnessed how He's used it as a conduit of wisdom for me and mine.

While there is no one universally agreed upon "Christian" way to educate a child, God continues to use these summertime Scriptures as arrows to point me to my good work. When the honeymoon phase of a fresh new year gives way to the daily grind, I cry out to Him for *rhema* words, and He provides them in generous helpings. I then press forward, bolstered and confident in my calling.

> If you ask for wisdom for your child's education, God will give it abundantly—no secret codes or special security clearance required.

God does not withhold His will from me, and He won't withhold it from you, friend. If you ask for wisdom for your child's education, He will give it abundantly— no secret codes or special security clearance required. Immerse yourself in Scripture, and it will become a compass, guiding you toward True North. His *rhema* will answer your heart cries and cast out your fears. What once looked like a coincidence will begin to show itself for what it's been all along, God's calling.

3

The Path to Bravery

Bravery. There's an essential oil for that, right—some modern-day elixir or formula designed to bolster your confidence and help you do this homeschooling thing like a momma-warrior? Well, that would be the easy fix, wouldn't it? I think we all know, however, that you can't bottle bravery or squeeze it into some shiny shrink-wrap. Bravery can't be found in a twelve-step program with celebrity endorsements. No, bravery doesn't come by way of any of those. The path to brave isn't immediate, but it is lasting if you follow it all the way to the end.

Since you've turned the page, I'm going to assume that you see your decision to homeschool, no matter how it came about, as a calling from God. Because of that, you've decided to tiptoe onward, but you're still stuck on the first leg of the journey: fear. That's quite all right. Every race has to have a starting line. But you can't remain there, especially if you've been homeschooling for any length of time. Just as a runner's muscles would eventually atrophy if he stayed in that bent starting position forever, your homeschool is doomed to failure if you never move past fear. So how do you start?

Know What Fear Is

Typically, the more you sit in fear, the more you fear it. You become paralyzed by your fear of fear. You convince yourself you'll never find bravery, and that negative self-talk anchors you, dragging you further and further down an ever-deepening pit. In truth, this fear of fear usually comes from a misunderstanding of what fear actually is.

So often in Christian circles, all fear is painted as sin; as the opposite of trust in God. But fear is not the opposite of trust, and certainly not all fear is sin. Some fear is actually a healthy, God-made emotion given to humanity for our own good. Without it, we would have no common sense. But fear can't be permanent. It was only meant as a temporary caution, a temporary fix, a momentary remedy. Eventually, fear will propel you to fight or flight. You'll either have to flee your fears of homeschooling or face them.

Fleeing is the easy way out, of course. Running the other direction from something often produces instant calm and immediate safety, but fleeing doesn't usually make the difficult thing go away. It just ignores it. In the end, you'll have to make a choice: *Will I face this obstacle, or will I sit forever in status quo?* Both sides of the question are scary, so your answer will have to depend on which fear you fear most. In that way, fear is a great motivator. It propels action. When given the choice between what *is* and what *can be*, bravery chooses the latter, and that makes all the difference.

Since you're homeschooling, there was probably something about the status quo—the public or private school options available—that you fear, or at least don't like. And since you're reading this book, I'm also going to assume that you fear homeschool failure. Which fear do you fear most?

I know it's scary to trust God with your child's uncertain future. But that's just it: the future might look murky and unknown to you, but it is completely known to God. Even when all the pieces of homeschooling haven't fallen into place yet, you can trust that they will eventually. God, in His providential plan, can use your fears to bring about abundantly more than you could ever ask or imagine in your homeschool (Eph. 3:20).

I'm not just tossing out platitudes and epithets here. I've experienced God's abundantly more plans in my own homeschool time and time again. In fact, just recently His more came covered in skin and wearing a welcoming smile. His more in my less was named Jacqui.

Jacqui is a financial advisor by day and a homeschooling mother by later-in-the-day. Last year, she sent out an email to a handful of homeschool moms in our area announcing that she would be offering an algebra class to any interested students. Her simple offering made me tear up. Even before I had finished reading her message, I was in a full-on ugly cry.

You see, in 2008, two years before I even met Jacqui, I harbored a secret fear. My daughter was supposed to be starting kindergarten that coming fall. And while I really had an urge to homeschool her, I knew she wouldn't stay little for very long and would one day need to learn difficult things like algebra. I also knew that numbers and I have always had a blood feud. Math is dead to me. It's bad enough that it gets all of the numbers. But then, somewhere around sixth grade, it starts stealing all the letters too. (Bad form, Math. Stick to your side of the playground, and let me stick to mine.)

I knew even way back when my daughter was in kindergarten and just learning to count that someday I'd need God to do something big in our homeschool to get me through. I'd need abundantly more. I did not know how or when He would fill in the gap, but I knew He would. If He was truly calling me to homeschool, He would provide the means for me to do it, even math. My fear was not a sin, but my disobedience in my fear would have been. God in His loving compassion for me provided not only an algebra teacher but also a treasured friend. If I had chosen not to homeschool all those years ago, I would have missed out on both.

As a homeschooling mom, it's natural to want to cower in your shortcomings. When you feel ill-equipped or average, it's easy to let fear make you want to cling to safety. But what if all your fears are what God will use to lead you toward the big things He has in store for you and your kids?

What if all your fears are what God will use to lead you toward the big things He has in store for you and your kids?

Know Who You Are

Like fear, sometimes that word *average* keeps us bolted in place; keeps us from doing the hard things. But *average* is a word that the world contrived. It has never been in God's vocabulary. He uses words like *good* and *beloved, heir* and *chosen*. Average is a measurement used to push down, hold back, and leave out. But to God, you are never just an acceptable homeschool mom; you are always accepted. You are pre-approved. You are fully known and fully loved.

The world will always tell an "average" mother that she cannot teach her children well because the world will always look for qualifications, accolades, and proofs of her abilities. The world will always operate from a bracket system. It will always keep score and contend for position. But unlike that of the world, God's opinion of you is not based on what you have accomplished. He's not concerned with who you are—your status or ranking among humankind. He cares more about whose you are. He looks to your identity in Christ, not your merits. Your value and worth have nothing to do with your ability, but everything to do with His.

According to the world's estimation, you might be quite average, perhaps even "unable" and "unqualified" to teach your children. That diagnosis might be the water that feeds your fear, growing deep roots of trembling and trepidation. Remember though, fear is not always a sin. It's only when you stay stagnate and still in your fear that a healthy, God-made emotion becomes bent by the Enemy.

Since the very beginning, Satan has taken the self-doubt of humanity, coupled it with some truth, and slipped in an itty-bitty lie when no one was looking in order to dupe entire generations into believing God will never give a Christian any more than she can handle on her own. In this case, he'd like you to believe that if you were called to homeschooling it was because God knew you could do it—and so you better come through.

Satan wants nothing more than for you to pull yourself up by your bootstraps and try to get this thing done all on your own. Then when you trip over your first hurdle and find yourself face down in despair, you'll begin to question. You'll begin to doubt. Your doubt will lead to defeat, and he'll stand by with a smug smile winning the day. But the very idea that you can "handle" anything on your own is a sad bit of Christianese that has been passed around the Body like last year's sinus infection at the annual church potluck. That notion is not found anywhere in Scripture. In fact, it's the very antithesis of God's Word as it misrepresents the gospel.

If you could somehow muster up enough skill, or put in enough time, or push forward with more effort to overcome the hard parts of homeschooling (or anything for that matter), if you

God didn't call you to homeschooling because *you* could handle it. He called you because *He* could handle it.

could somehow do this thing in your own strength, what would be the need of a Savior? What would be the point of Christ's coming? No, my friend, God didn't call you to homeschooling because *you* could handle it. He called you because *He* could handle it.

More often than not, God calls us to do hard things not *despite* the fact that they will be tough, but *because* they will be tough. Does this sound a little half-baked to you? It often does to me too. Let me spin it for you this way. Instead of quietly hiding in your fears of homeschooling, what if you admitted them? What if you finally came to the end of *your* ability and handed it all off to God? What if you gave voice to all your inadequacies and held them out to the Savior?

Sometimes we're afraid to admit our anxieties, as if God doesn't know them already. It's okay to say that you're not okay. Admitting your concerns, your insecurities, and even your disappointments about home education to God isn't a sign of disobedience or disrespect. It's a sign of trust. It's an indication that you know He's big enough, even for this. Even a *Why?* can be worshipful when it's brought to the One who can answer it best.

What would happen if you finally confessed your worries about homeschooling and gave God control? Well, as Scripture says, He will draw near to you as you draw near to Him (James 4:8). When you finally hand Him the reins, step back, and let Him do His thing, you'll watch your liabilities become your greatest assets. His power will be made perfect in your weakness (2 Cor. 12:9). As you decrease, He will increase (John 3:30). Knowing that, why in the world would you ever want to just sit silently in your fear? Why would you insist on attempting to teach your kids on your own? You don't have to answer that. I know why, because I do it too.

You don't have to fear your inabilities or inadequacies to homeschool. What you see as a fault or a failure could actually be the very thing that God wants to use to get you to admit you can't do it on your own. It might be what He wants to employ to draw you to Himself, the only One who can.

God is at work right now in the midst of your fear to break your bonds of self-sufficiency. He might be amplifying your homeschooling defi- ciencies in order for you to finally admit who you really are—just a regular mom who, in and of herself, cannot homeschool her children well, a mother who is unprepared for the job. Relin- quishing control of your child's education to God and admitting you need Him is one more step to- ward bravery.

> God is at work right now in the midst of your fear to break your bonds of self-sufficiency.

Know Who God Is

In full disclosure, when you admit to the world you can't home-school and finally point to the One who can, you might receive contemptuous looks and wagging fingers. It's only natural. The world doesn't understand an intimate faith in something it can't see. But that's the beauty of faith. There's an element of unknown, of risk, to it. The thing is, as popular author and speaker Holley Gerth once wrote, "Faith without risk isn't faith. It's just facts."[1] Do you have faith enough to trust God with your children— not just with their eternal forevers, but also with their here-and-nows? Faith doesn't eliminate fear, mind you; it just overcomes it. It acknowledges that you know who God is and that He alone is able to steer your child's education in the way it should go.

Perhaps 1 Corinthians 1:25–29 explains it best. It reads,

> For the foolishness of God is wiser than men, and the weak-
> ness of God is stronger than men.

For consider your calling, brothers: not many of you were wise according to worldly standards, not many were powerful, not many were of noble birth. But God chose what is foolish in the world to shame the wise; God chose what is weak in the world to shame the strong; God chose what is low and despised in the world, even things that are not, to bring to nothing things that are, so that no human being might boast in the presence of God.

God is in the business of calling foolish, simple people to do great and mighty things—not because *they* are able, but because *He* is. In doing so, He stands to gain the most glory. He gets to wave His banner of victory.

If your calling to homeschool was doable and if all the columns added up, you'd be tempted to climb up on a platform of your own making and receive the applause of the world. But since your calling is out of reach, then the victory will go to God. Your glaring inadequacies will only stand to prove His might. All who witness the end result will, as Psalm 26:7 says, recount His wondrous deeds. You'll only be a side note in the story, a bit part in the grand performance.

Bravery comes when you know who God is: *Jehovah-nissi*, a banner who goes before and behind you, securing a victory. It comes when you do your bit part in obedience and let God do the rest. Will you do everything perfectly? No. But even if you end up doing a whole lot of wrong in your attempts to do something right in homeschooling, God is content and able to sort out the results.

Whether you want to acknowledge it or not, your doubt is like a small fist of defiance raised to God. In your doubt, you quietly question if He is really good and if you can really trust Him. But He is good and, what's more, He loves your kids more than you do. Unlike your love for them, His love is unwavering and immovable. The best part about a fixed love is that it is never dependent upon your ability. So whether you can teach or you can't, whether you graduated summa cum laude from an Ivy League school or barely eked past twelfth grade, whether you can juggle teaching your older kids and nursing a baby at the same time, you can trust that God will be good to your kids. He is good, and His love endures forever (Ps. 107:1).

You can't mess up that goodness. You can't add or detract from that love. As a homeschool mom who often feels like her life is like a ride on a giant tilt-a-whirl, you should feel relieved to know that nothing you do or don't do will make God love your children more; on the flip side, nothing you do or don't do will make Him love them any less.

Rest in that perfect love. As 1 John 4:18 reminds us, it can cast out your fears. Perfect love can be trusted, and so can the Giver of that love. When you fix your mind on Him and trust in His plan, He promises perfect peace (Isa. 26:3–4). He is big enough to hold up your homeschool, even when you can't.

All those years ago, when I knew I couldn't hold up algebra, I was faced with two choices: I could cave to my fear of numbers and send my daughter to a traditional school, dismissing the very clear tug I was feeling toward homeschooling, or I could just obey in faith, knowing that while the way wouldn't be easy, God would provide what my daughter needed when she needed it. I, obviously, chose option number two. But what if I hadn't?

The scenario probably would have gone something like this: I would have sent her to the brick-and-mortar school down the street. And when the time came, the "experts" would have taught her what *x* equals. She'd learn it. She'd graduate. The end. But in following that smooth road, we both would have missed *abundantly more*. The same is true if God had revealed His ultimate plan right from the very beginning of our homeschooling journey, way back when Maddie was just learning to count.

If I would have met my friend Jacqui the summer before I started homeschooling and if she would have declared her desire to teach an algebra class someday, I would've launched into homeschool with absolute certainty. I would have skipped the doubts and fears and looked to the future with ease. There would have been no need for me to trust, no need for me to pray, no need for me to lean into the promises of Philippians 1:6 and ultimately into Him. And in the end, *that* was the biggest *more* of all—that in the waiting and the wondering, I drew closer to Him; that I clung tighter and trusted longer, and my daughter did too.

At the end of the day, God's *abundantly more* is always found in our relationship with Him and how our lives can bring Him glory. While earning an *A* in algebra was a piece of the story God had for my girl that year, it wasn't the *more*. It was just a bonus—the cherry on top. The real *more* was what He did in her heart and in mine. Right smack dab in the middle of the fear, we had to press hard into God. We had nothing else to turn to—not our abilities, not our resources, not our plans. And when we came to the end of *us*, we saw God. Without the fear, we would have missed His presence entirely. We wouldn't have been looking for it. We wouldn't have been waiting expectantly for it.

It's All About Perspective

Nothing will put you on the fast track to bravery quite like acknowledging who you are versus who God is. That kind of truthful assessment will give you the proper perspective of your calling, no matter how difficult the task might seem.

Homeschooling can be scary, it's true. But use that fear; leverage it for success. Allow your fear to be a firm reminder of your only source of victory—God. Allow His resolve to strengthen yours. If I were a betting woman, I'd place my money on His clear call to you, every time. At the risk of painting God with a human brush, I have a sneaking suspicion that when He called you to homeschooling, He did so with confidence. He didn't stand there fumbling over the pronunciation of your name like your high school gym teacher on the first day of roll call. He shouted it with boldness.

Homeschool with that same kind of fervor. Don't be scared. Be brave. *Scared* is just the mask that fear wears to lure a mom into defeat—and defeat never comes from God. Bravery, on the other hand, admits not only who you are, but also who God is. *Brave* shifts the confidence to God and fully embraces His ability to do it right. Do it well. Do it for your good. God chose you for this task, so don't question His ability to choose wisely.

Every time you feel the clutching grasp of fear wrap around your thoughts, bring your fears to Him. Lay them out in faith—not with your pretty Sunday School faith or your good-girl Bible study faith, but with your everyday faith that is real and raw and true. Don't try to hide behind a brave face. Remember, God has seen scared before. This ain't His first rodeo. You won't fool Him with your makeshift armor of fluffy prayers and spiritual checklists. Admit you are afraid. Then be willing to homeschool afraid, if you must, fully knowing that faith does not eliminate fear, it just knows who to give the fear to at the end of the day.

> *If God has led you to homeschool then you are compelled to walk in faith, not fear. Faith recognizes God is bigger than any challenge life sends, including homeschooling.*[2]
> CINDY ROLLINS
> author of *Mere Motherhood*

It just insists that you do the thing even while you're shaking.

Each small step of faith will give you a better, more accurate view of the list of "impossibles" that plague the secret spaces of your mind. With the proper perspective of all of these, you'll be like the young David when he faced the mighty Philistine

Goliath in the valley so many years ago (1 Sam. 17).

Twice a day for the forty days leading up to David's arrival, the giant Goliath had taunted God's army, terrorizing them and drawing the battle to a standoff. But when all the trained Israelite soldiers stood paralyzed in fear, David was moved to action. What looked like sure defeat to everyone else was a victory already won in David's eyes. Why? Because while all others saw a Titan too big and unconquerable, David's simple faith made him see an obstacle so huge that it was impossible to miss. With each small step toward his foe, David's faith was proved. He saw past the giant in front of him and looked to his God who was bigger. And that perspective made all the difference.

The Goliath-size task of homeschooling might look overwhelming and impossible right now because the journey is long and the final destination unsure. But as you trust God with your small stones and begin to wield them in faith, you'll start to form a new perspective. The time spent encouraging the strong-willed child to do her work will prove to be an opportunity for God to sand off the rough places of her character. The cold war that started when your extended family learned of your decision to homeschool will become a chance to show your kids how to restore relationships with grit and grace. And your very real algebra allergy could end up drawing you closer and closer to Christ. Obedience will help you grow a new perspective.

As you continue to take steps toward the impossible, your knees might be knocking, and that's okay. Just muster up enough courage to ignore the "Take care" and "Be safe" messages of this world. Then move one more inch forward. Eventually, the victory will begin to feel like the sure bet that it is. Let your fear push you toward the hard things of homeschooling by pushing your homeschooling right toward God—the one, true path to bravery.

4

Watch Your Own Dice

L ast September, my family and I went on a three-day camping trip in the northern wilderness of Minnesota. My husband is typically a tent or backpack-only kind of camper. But I somehow convinced him to rent a bunkhouse from a Christian camp for this particular outing.

This was no luxury lodge, mind you. It was a simple log room with four pallet-style bunk beds on one end and a rickety table and chairs at the other. The only other furnishings to be found were mismatched curtains and a thick layer of dirt on the hardwood floor. While my wilderness man was not thrilled about the set-up, he could easily see that a bunkhouse was the best place for a former city girl and all her children to gently shake hands with nature.

We spent the first full day outdoors, living wild and free. But by nightfall, my crew was physically spent. We had moved our bodies all day long and needed to still them. I herded them inside and unpacked a few card games as well as a dice game we'd never played before, Tenzi, and set them all out on the table for the family to play in turn.

Not surprisingly, the children chose to play the raucous dice game first versus the pack of sedate cards. (Even late at night, my children have a habit of choosing *noise* over *nestle*. So much for still bodies.) We spread out on the dirt-covered floor and began playing. Everyone was given a set of ten colored dice with which to roll in hopes of creating a Yahtzee-style match before anyone else did.

After we'd played several rounds, I began to notice that my middle son, Finn, was becoming frustrated. He began heaving great sighs and slamming his dice down at the end of each round. Sighs became groans, which eventually morphed into growls. By the end of one heated match, he was in tears.

"Can we play something else?" he asked through his sobs. "Everyone has won lots of rounds, and I have lost every single time."

It was true. He had lost time and time again. In fact, he had done so poorly throughout each and every round that he never had a chance of even coming close to winning. While I did not condone his poor sportsmanship, I could understand his frustration. What I couldn't understand was *why* he continued to lose. It was a game of pure chance. Victory had nothing to do with skill, age, or logic. Even my then three-year-old had won a few times. Statistically speaking, Finn should have won at least once, but he hadn't. It just didn't make sense.

"Why don't we play one more time?" I suggested in hopes that I could somehow Sherlock Holmes my way to an answer for this game night mystery.

As we played the final round, I went through the motions: roll, select, roll again, but my focus was not on winning. My hands may have been shaking dice, but my eyes were set on Finn. By the second roll of the round, it was easy to see why he had lost every single game that night. He wasn't watching his own dice.

Instead of looking down in front of him to see what he had rolled and to determine his next move, each time he shook out his set, he looked around the room at everyone else's collection of dice. He watched to see if someone was close to winning. His gaze scanned the floor from one set of dice to another, wasting precious rolling time. Most players had rolled three or four times before he picked up his dice to make his second roll. By taking his eyes off his own dice, he had crippled his own chances of ever winning a round.

"Tenzi!" someone yelled, declaring victory and ending the game. With that, Finn was a puddle of tears once again.

"Watch your own dice, Finn," I gently instructed him. "You lost because you never kept your eyes on your own dice. You were so concerned with what everyone else was rolling that you wasted your rolling time. You'll never win if you don't watch your own dice." That's true of Tenzi, but it's also true of homeschooling.

When Your Focus Gets Out of Focus

So often we homeschool mothers take our eyes off of our own dice—the unique home God has given us and the call He has placed in our lives. In doing so, we lose. Bravery is displaced by fear because our focus gets out of focus.

Admittedly, it's easy to lose focus. We live in an age when "the Joneses" don't just live next door. They live on our laptops, in our phones, and in our earbuds. We can't shake them. They are always there, right in front of us, making our twenty-first-century living very crowded. Our lives are busy, and with the steady barrage of media, our lives are also very noisy. "Keeping up" feels unavoidable. Before we lay all the blame on our digital devils, however, let's first recognize that social media is not the only cause for blame. It is just a tool, after all, but like most useful tools this side of eternity, it is often hijacked by Satan.

The constant stream of pressure poured out on social media has us all convinced that we're not doing enough, we're not organized enough, we're not fill-in-the-blank enough. The clamor of Facebook, Instagram, and Pinterest is a never-ending parade of perfection. So often we see only the highlight reels of a person's life—the ideal days, the obedient kids, the flawless homes. All the gritty parts get meticulously edited, and what's left looks magical because life always looks better through photo filters. We place someone else's extraordinary over our everyday and begin to feel underwhelmed with our lives and ourselves.

In the realm of homeschooling, this social-media-fueled pressure can feel particularly pronounced. Because we're at home most of the time, it's easy to pop onto Facebook three or three hundred times a day. It's often our one-and-only access to the outside world, after all. Once there, we see not only all the *must-do* parenting posts and pins, but also all the homeschooling ones. Simple math shows that as homeschool-ers, we can earn ourselves a double portion of mommy guilt. Not to mention the fact that it's all too tempting to use Facebook and In-stagram as a bullhorn—to shout and show the world all the grand and glorious things our kids are doing as a way to validate our decision to all the naysayers.

> In the realm of homeschooling, social-media-fueled pressure can feel particularly pronounced.

When you begin to homeschool, you might start out rolling your own dice with intensity, but then you get distracted and take your eyes off what's right in front of you. You look at how everyone else is homeschooling—you see their picturesque suc-cess and assume that if you just followed their magic formula, your homeschool would turn out exactly like theirs. You invest in yet another pricey new curriculum you can't afford because that one blog post has you believing the shelves of books you already own just won't cut it; you make the salt dough map of Europe because that one Pinterest pin said it was one of ten *must-do* history projects for homeschoolers even though your children would rather just draw it in colored pencils; and you put your kids into multiple extracurricular activities you don't have time for in order to keep up with the Harvard-bound kids in that one article you read.

Don't misunderstand me: wanting to provide the very best education for your kids is not, in and of itself, wrong. Your chil-

> *To homeschool bravely means to homeschool without the weight of comparison. It is being able to look at what your neighbor is doing, be inspired by it, gather ideas, and then do your own thing without feelings of guilt, inadequacy, or comparison. If the mom down the street homeschools in a skirt, apron, and pearls, and you never leave your yoga pants, either change clothes or own it. Homeschooling bravely is not being a victim—even to your own fears.*[1]
>
> PAM BARNHILL
>
> author of *Better Together* and host of the *Your Morning Basket Podcast*

dren are one of the most important "talents" that God has entrusted to you (Matt. 25). Stewarding their education well is not sinful, but a desperate grasp for perfection is. It's a selfish attempt to build your own little kingdom void of God's help. And let's face it, seeking perfection usually just leads to paralysis. If you're like most people, when you see that perfection is an unattainable finish line, you give up. You throw in the towel and assume it just can't be done. But isn't imperfect progress better than no progress at all? Slow-and-steady forward motion will get 'er done faster than an unrealized good intention every time.

The fishbowl living of social media has put an entirely new spin on "keeping up with the Joneses." It's made it all too easy to lay someone else's perfectly contrived picture over your home like a template. But you can't just copy-paste your way to success.

God doesn't want—or expect—you to do homeschool like the elusive Jones family. He didn't give you the same tools that He gave them, so He doesn't expect you to build the same thing. You have unique gifts, time, and talents. You have unmatched children with one-of-a-kind interests. You have a singular budget with a desire to spend it in a specific way. Everything about you and yours is exclusive. No matter how hard you try to mirror the educational journey of someone else, you will never see the same outcome. What you'll end up with instead is a life of discouragement. You'll always come up short. You'll never "keep up."

My homeschool isn't supposed to look like yours, and yours isn't supposed to look like mine. Don't read one more word of this book until you fully embrace that truth. Otherwise, you'll constantly get sidetracked by the successes of others. Instead of just rejoicing with those who rejoice, as Scripture says, you'll become bitter (Rom. 12:15). Deep seeds of jealousy will take root, forcing their way up into your everyday decisions. What seemed like a good choice at the beginning of the school year will suddenly seem subpar. The progress you saw in your children just yesterday will begin to look like decline today. Gratitude will morph into discontent, and you'll spin yourself into a tizzy trying to renovate your entire school year. You'll continue to add more to your plate, and in the end, you'll divide your time, energy, resources, and talent. You'll end up with a homeschool defined by average because you'll have taken your eyes off the things that really matter—the dice you've been given.

What's Your Awesome?

For the most part, this social media thing is just an illusion anyway. Facebook, Instagram, and—dare I say it—mommy blogs are all curators of "awesome." When you look at the collective perfection of everyone online, it's natural to inadvertently lump all of that awesome onto one imaginary person, to forget that each of those amazing photos, musings, and memes have all come from *different* women. You might even find yourself believing that *everyone* is awesome at all of those things and that, because you're not, you somehow fall short. But the truth is, most of us are just awesome at one or two things and pretty mediocre at all the rest.

Sadly, I was deep into my thirties before I ever saw social media for what it truly is: smoke and mirrors. Last year, I read a book by a well-known mommy-finance blogger and homeschooler. I'd followed her blog for years and had, unfortunately, fallen prey to the comparison trap while reading it, more times than I care to admit. On the fourteen-inch screen, she came across as a Mary Poppins 2.0. You know the type: practically perfect in every way. Then I read her book. It was a game changer for me, but not because it offered great tips on organization, which it did. In fact, it was chock full of all that and more. Ironically, though, that's not what made the book so life-giving to me.

I glossed over the pages and pages that detailed what this mom *does* with her time and energy and focused my lens on the two or three paragraphs that told what she *does not* do. In the very first chapter, she confessed that she does not do a lot of cooking but chooses to eat out a few times a week instead; she hires a maid service on occasion; and she has a team of people to help behind-the-scenes with her blog. Please don't think I'm judging her in this. On the contrary, I say kudos to her for being smart enough to whisper a *no* to some things in her life in order to have space and time to shout *yes* to all the rest.

After reading that small list of disclosures, I wasn't sure if I should cry out of relief—mascara running and everything—or begin the slow clap, building to a crescendo. Her words were so transforming. You see, I had created this unnatural illusion of her in my head. It was a spotted-unicorn kind of fantasy that was one part her, one part me, and one part every-great-homeschooling-mother-I-had-ever-met. I assumed that in addition to finding the time to be uber-organized and financially savvy, she *also* managed to accomplish all the other areas of life with an equal amount of *awesome*. I knew I cooked every single meal *my* family ate, cleaned all the nooks and crannies of *my* little cottage, handled all the business of *my* blog, and concluded she must do all of that as well. But she doesn't. My misplaced neurosis was not in any way *her* doing, mind you. No, that crazy-train was all completely conducted by yours truly. I took her highlight reels and measured them against my *everyday* life. I watched her dice, assuming they were exactly like mine.

The fact of the matter is, I'm pretty underwhelming at most things and a hot mess of chaos at everything else. I'm almost always late—to everything. I can never find my cell phone even though I'd take a blood oath that I put it back in the exact same spot every time. I have a kitchen drawer that is the Bermuda Triangle of spice jars, and I'm pretty sure that if I forget to show up to one more chiropractor appointment, my doctor is going to file a missing person's report.

But . . . while I can make mediocrity look like an Olympic sport in some areas of my life, I'm pretty awesome in others. Everyone's awesome at *something*. That's true for me, and it's true for you. If I stop to compare any area of my life to someone else's, especially homeschooling, I can easily get discouraged. *Average* isn't very motivating. So I choose not to focus on all those so-so parts and set my sights on my *awesome* instead. *Awesome* is contagious. When I consciously acknowledge my *awesome*, I start to see it grow. By amplifying the exceptional parts of my homeschool, I take the spotlight off of all the less satisfying parts. In doing so, I'm not trying to forget or dismiss my struggles. I'm just not letting them commandeer my thoughts. I'm not allowing negative self-talk to steer my decisions.

After reading that blogger's book and running face-first into the truth about social media, I sat down to create a list of things I can do well in my homeschool. I had spent far too much time mentally cataloging all the ways I was failing, so I thought it might be time to come at personal assessment from a different angle. My list went something like this: I can create a unit study like a boss, I'm a stellar paper organizer, and I've got this whole reading-aloud-with-funny-accents thing under control. Admittedly, an "awesome list" seems like an exercise in narcissism. Was I just trying to pad my resume to make myself feel better? Perhaps I was at first, but as I looked over the list, I began to see the real Person behind all that *awesome*. It wasn't me. It was God. He is the Giver of every perfect gift, including any good gift I can hold out to my homeschool (James 1:17). I can create great unit studies, but only because He has given me the desire, knowledge, and budget to do so. I can organize paper, but only because He has wired my brain to think in columns and categories. I can read with a British lilt, but only because He has gifted me with a flair for theatrics. (I'm pretty sure drama is my superpower.) These are my dice. This is what God has given me.

What about you? What is your *awesome*? Stop right now and make a mental list of the good gifts God has given you. Better yet, write them down in gratitude. The next time you start to feel the pressure of *average*, look to your list. Acknowledge that you might be mediocre at some things, but then be willing to see and celebrate all the rest. Point the spotlight on the good dice God has given you. In doing so, you'll be taking the attention off the "awesome" illusion created by social media and our competitive culture and putting it where it truly belongs, on Him.

> Acknowledge that you might be mediocre at some things, then be willing to see and celebrate all the rest. Point the spotlight on the good dice God has given you.

A + B Homeschooling

Sorry to say, iPads and iPhones aren't the only *I*'s that sneak in to take our focus off of our own dice. While it's easy to point the finger of guilt at Facebook, or Instagram, or Pinterest, sometimes the problem isn't any of these. Sometimes the problem is us—you and me. Too often our sight gets moved because of an unholy trinity of me, myself, and I. If you're like most women, myself included, you are probably your worst enemy.

When God called you to homeschool, His request was simple: to teach your children His commandments when you sit in the house, when you walk by the way, when you lie down, and when you rise (Deut. 6:7). Sometimes, though, His clear instruction just to teach through living seems too easy, as if there should be more to it. In an effort to cover all the bases, you create some complicated equation to produce homeschooling perfection. You begin to add spelling bee competitions, Latin verb conjugations, Ivy-League-university-recommended reading lists, and so much more to the easy instructions of Deuteronomy 6:7 because if God said *A* was good, then certainly *A+B* would be even better, right?

According to a business analysis published by Marketdata Enterprises, an independent Tampa-based research firm, the self-improvement industry in the U.S. is worth an estimated $11 billion.[2] While the homeschool portion of those billions is rather small, there's a significant amount of pressure coming from that little piece of the pie all dedicated to the idea that if you just knew the right methods, used the right curriculum, went to the right conferences, and did the prescribed 10 Must-Do science projects, you could create homeschool heaven. Your children would grow up to be happy, healthy, productive members of society.

Suddenly God's simple call to teach your kids His way becomes a three-ring circus. You add to it and add to it and add to it until it is barely recognizable. You rush about like a hamster on a wheel, expelling a lot of energy, creating tally marks trying to look good to all the naysayers and be "enough" in their eyes. But you'll never get anywhere with that kind of action. The moment you stop performing, you'll be right back where you started from because the truth is, no matter where you draw a line of "perfection," there will always be someone who thinks it should be moved elsewhere. No matter how much you add to your homeschool day, there will always be something else that could be added.

Don't misunderstand me. There's nothing wrong with enrolling your budding thespian in a community theater performance of *Hamlet* or teaching French to your six-year-old, but only if you're doing it because you feel like it's a part of God's big story for that child. If, on the other hand, you're piling on a heap of extras simply out of obligation or to impress others, you are committing spiritual adultery. You're clamoring for approval from everybody else and coveting the home, talents, children, husband, and budget they have, assuming that if you just had all of those things, you could surely homeschool well. You are misplacing your focus and forgetting all about the "Well done" that matters most (Matt. 25:21).

What you may not realize is that in attempting to *A+B* your homeschool, you are spending far too much time worshipping the homeschool mom you think you're supposed to be instead of opening your arms wide to the homeschool mom He has made you to be.

That's the very problem with living under the guilt of someone else's law and not the grace of Christ's love. If you see yourself as a homeschool failure, ultimately you will be driven by guilt and crushed by shame. That kind of life is certainly not of God. But, if by some slim chance you see yourself as a homeschool success, you will be overcome with pride, and that's also not of God. In trying to obey all of the human-made educational laws and the expectations of others, you'll become spiritually anemic, void of the life-giving promise God gave you and your kids in Philippians 1:6—that He will finish the good work He started in you and in them.

Don't think for a moment you're alone in your *A+B* efforts. I've grown pale-white in my need to please. That's why I'm so glad that Jesus has given us the cure for our self-inflicted anemia in Matthew 11:28–30. He says, "Come to me, all who labor and are heavy laden, and I will give you rest. Take my yoke upon you, and learn from me, for I am gentle and lowly in heart, and you will find rest for your souls. For my yoke is easy and my burden is light." His yoke *is* easy—you are to teach His way—"when you sit in your house, and when you walk by the way, and when you lie down, and when you rise" (Deut. 6:7). That's it. A light burden. It only becomes heavy when you start adding to it.

Looking back at that chaotic game of Tenzi last fall, I can see clearly the path of failure for my son. He continued to lose game after game because he took his eyes off of his own dice. He was so concerned with how everyone else was playing that he wasted precious time. He may have had a winning handful of dice, but he lost every round. Each time he cast his gaze on someone else's success, fear slipped in and he began to lose.

If you're fearful, Homeschool Mama, perhaps it's because you've allowed something to steal your gaze away from your own dice. Perhaps you've begun to look outside of your gifts and passions and have brought your eyes to someone else's methods, someone else's calling, someone else's children. The truth is, you will never learn to homeschool bravely until you take your eyes off social media, set them on Christ and the *awesome* He has given you, and invest your time in the simple instructions for teaching that God laid out long ago. These are your dice. Watch them well.

PART 2

The Struggle

For every little part of your child's life you try to own and fix for them, you are taking away something from the work and worth of God in their lives.

———————————————

SEPTEMBER MCCARTHY

Why Motherhood Matters

5

When You Have
One of *Those* Kids

Perhaps you are among the 107 percent of homeschool mothers who have one of *those* kids—a difficult child who doesn't want to color inside societal lines. Homeschooling this wild one feels like you've been thrown into the deep end of the pool before you've had a chance to learn to swim. You're just dog-paddling, trying to stay alive. I've been there. I'm still there some days, but not every day. My homeschooling journey with my strong one has taught me to view his spit-fire stubbornness in a different light.

Ever since Adam and Eve took the forbidden fruit, all of humanity has had a natural bent toward sin and toward a me-first attitude. That means you. That means your child. But as I've mentioned before, it's not by accident that *you* were given *this* child. There is something about your personality that he needs. And dare I say it, there's something about his personality that you need too.

Let me explain. You can easily shove your difficult one off on someone else eight hours a day. On the surface, the public school looks like the perfect exit strategy for your current daily hostage situation. Someone else would get to deal with the rabble-rouser, and you could enjoy a few hours of sanity with your other children. And as an added bonus, your strong-willed one would get an education in the deal too. What could be better than that? Public or private school is clearly a win-win, right?

Before you hitch your wagon to that logic, please acknowledge that admitting daytime defeat will always come with a catch. After school and on weekends, your child will set up camp on the couch, bringing his strong will home with him. You'll have all kinds of good intentions. *The short daily respite will surely provide a temporary truce in our home, offering just enough separation to make everyone play nicely once again*, you'll tell yourself. But despite your best efforts to create alliances during those non-school hours, things won't improve. Your child's willfulness will continue to ride shotgun, creating a nightly stand-off. Why? Because buildings don't ever get built on good intentions; they take construction, they take work. The same is true of character.

Ever since Adam and Eve took the forbidden fruit, all of humanity has had a natural bent toward sin and toward a me-first attitude. That means you. That means your child.

Your difficult child is a work in progress. All of his traits were woven and knit together by God, and they are good. Like with most things here on earth, however, the *good* that God created in him has been seized by sin, at least temporarily. But there's hope. Just like a piece of sand produces a pearl, the *wild* in your child can be the start of something great if it's given time and attention. That stubborn-streak that refuses to do what it's told to do when it's told to do it can one day be the iron will that stands against social injustice or political strong-arming. That argumentative tongue that wants to hiss and boo around the lunch table each afternoon might one day fight for Truth and defend the faith. That headstrong curiosity that dumps paint, sand, and glitter on your freshly shampooed carpet may one day discover, do, and create things the world has been anxiously waiting for. Your child is a sentence that is not yet complete. Don't anxiously put a period where God has only dropped a comma.

This brief moment of childhood is your time to play workman. God has given you this child so your love and gifts might help refine and mold him. "In every block of marble I see a statue as plain as though it stood before me, shaped and perfect in attitude and action. I have only to hew away the rough walls that imprison the lovely apparition to reveal it to the other eyes as mine see it," Michelangelo once said of his sculptures.[1] He could very well have been talking about your difficult child. When you look at your strong-willed one, you might only see a block of rough stone, but God sees a masterpiece. He wants to use you as a tool to chisel away the bits that aren't a part of the finished work He has planned. Did you catch that? He wants to use *you*. The key is to set your sights on who your child is becoming and not just how he is acting at this moment.

God is writing a story in the life of your child. And stories, at least the good ones, always have a beginning, a middle, and an end. It would be so much easier to skip to the last page—to the completed work. But by depositing your child into a desk down the street, you'd miss the work and your role in it. The middle pages are what make the last page so captivating. They're where

> Your child is a sentence that is not yet complete. Don't anxiously put a period where God has only dropped a comma.

all the action takes place. The pretty resolve is only pretty because of the struggle that happened just before it. To remove the struggle is to remove the story. That's not to belittle the struggle or to dismiss it away but to realize that the struggle is a necessary plot point in the bigger narrative. As Hebrews 5:14 tells us, maturity is learned through constant use. The struggle provides an opportunity to practice maturity.

> *You can't have virtue without trial; you can't have relationship without loyalty through good and bad; you can't have God's glory without giving up your own. It feels miserable in the moment, but the bad days are offerings of humility, something we give up to God and ask Him to do something with, even though they're terrible, rotten, no good. And He does.*[2]
> MYSTIE WINCKLER
> founder of SimplyConvivial.com

Are you willing to love in all the hard places? Willing to invest bit by tiny bit into your child's character? Willing to keep at it even when he's getting on your last blessed nerve? The process won't always be tidy, but it will be effective, in more ways than one. Here's a cold, hard reality: sometimes homeschooling is not about your children at all. Sometimes it is about you and what God seeks to do in your life. He wants to use everything about it, even your difficult child, to sand off your rugged edges. It's easy to assume that home is where your children learn to be more patient, more kind, more mature, more righteous. But don't forget, home is where you learn to become *more* too. As I mentioned, your difficult one is a work in progress, but so are you. Homeschooling with its oftentimes moment-by-complicated-moment investment can be one of the many tools God can use to bring you to completion. When He removes your ability to control all things by giving you a spirited child, you get thrust into deeper dependence upon Him.

This is not a child-rearing book, I'm not a counselor, and the verdict is still very much out on my own parenting— three very good reasons why I'm not going to give you a twelve-step action plan for raising your strong-willed child. Besides, heart issues require more than quick-fix solutions. Only the gospel can offer any real and lasting change. But may I offer you a few ideas that have helped to soften the prickly personalities in my home during the school day?

> Heart issues require more than quick-fix solutions.

Offer a Choice

Sometimes the crossed-arms of resistance are the quiet pleas of a child who just wants to be heard—to feel like a portion of his school day is within his control. Brainstorm ways you can re-linquish some of the decisions to him. Perhaps instead of doing every single review problem on the math page, he can choose to complete the even or odd numbered ones. Instead of writing a paragraph on birds as the curriculum dictates, allow him to select the topic he's most interested in. Skip over the assigned novel and gather a handful of titles from which he may choose to read in its place. Better yet, invite him to make a list of five to ten parts of the school day that he'd like to tweak, and do your best to honor those requests. Offering choice is not relinquishing your authority, it's just a loving way to welcome his input and include him in his own education.

By no means do you want to reward bad behavior. Sometimes a poor attitude is just *that*, a poor attitude, one that needs to be dealt with accordingly. But, just as you appreciate having a say in how your day runs, your child does too. Instead of always digging in your heels and matching will for will, I dare you to lend a listening ear. You might find that a soft answer really does turn away wrath and that your willingness to offer choice yields a truce in the daily struggle.

Establish Routines

Bad attitudes can sometimes grow out of a disordered day. Kids, especially, thrive under clear directions and expectations. Unfortunately, in their eagerness to start the school year each fall, many moms just *start* the school year. They plunge right into the books, projects, and math facts and forget that successful days are rooted in good routines and that those routines have to be taught and re-taught each and every year.

Nothing will derail a homeschool quite like allowing summertime habits to spill into the fall. In the summer, your kids may have a carefree schedule, a looser bedtime, and questionable eating habits. While a homeschool day should never be manhandled by a ticking clock, it does go so much smoother with a little more intentional rhythm. Everyone seems to walk more slowly and speak more kindly when they know what to expect.

Begin a few weeks before your planned first day of school and start establishing some good morning routines you can carry over to the busy school year. Get the kids up fifteen minutes earlier every few days until they are getting up before your intended learning time. Determine what personal hygiene and home-keeping tasks you'd like your kids to do before the start of each day. Make a list of these and set the list in a visible spot of your home. Train your kids to work their way down the list each morning. Sometimes it's helpful to serve breakfast only after all of the list items have been completed. In that way, breakfast becomes a built-in motivator and discourages sluggishness. Be sure to inspect what you expect, otherwise, any slight childish mediocrity will cause you more frustration. You'll find yourself wanting to kick kittens. It won't be pretty.

Also, begin transitioning to a more rigid chore schedule, assigning age-appropriate home (sweeping, sorting laundry, washing dishes, etc.) and school (sharpening pencils, putting school shelves in order, gathering library books, etc.) jobs to each of your kids. By teaching these skills before the school year begins, you will not only ensure a more efficient use of your school calendar, but you will also lighten your own school day workload by deferring some of the home-keeping duties to your kids.

With the exception of actual learning activities like completing worksheets and reading textbooks, begin to walk through the school day enforcing a more organized timeline. Practice these routines for several weeks at the end of summer. This will help realign your daily schedule, making it easier to just plug "school" into it when the time comes.

If you've already started the school year, don't be afraid to scale academics back for a few days in order to establish better habits. Make a list of the trouble spots of the day—times when chaos multiplies or attitudes flare. Spend some time brainstorming routines that could help you smooth out the day. Where would you like your kids to place their completed work each day—papers that need your once-over? What about school supplies? Where should those be stored during non-school hours? When the phone rings, what do you want the kids to be doing while you answer the call? Create action plans for the predictable so that you'll have wiggle room for the unpredictable.

You can't just assume your kids will naturally know how to start the school day well or how to use their time wisely. You have to teach them. Once you do, you'll find that a large majority of the day will be spent on autopilot, requiring little to no thought. Good habits will ensure that the bulk of your day is lather-rinse-repeat with no extra stress and no extra burden on you or them.

"Soft Open" the School Year

Don't expect your difficult child to go from 0 to 60 on that first day or even that first week. Give him grace. And while you're at it, give yourself some too. Plan for it. Require it. Create a first week (or even a first month) schedule that helps both of you transition into the full school day softly.

I've never started the homeschool year with a full load of kids and classes. Not ever. In the same way that a juggler tosses one new ball into his act at a time lest he drop the entire armload before he even begins, I always get one child launched before I add in the next one. I let each of my kids have their own first day of school. I usually start with my youngest child on a Monday. He does his core subjects like math, language, and handwriting, and the rest of the family celebrates him with all the typical fanfare that comes with a special *first*. And then he gets to take the rest of the week off while I move on to my next-oldest child. By the end of the week, each of my kids has had a chance to be celebrated, and I've slowly ramped up to a more difficult school load. The following Monday we are all a bit more prepared to spin the plates of a full day.

Some moms like to start with only one subject per child on the first day and then slowly add in another one with each subsequent day. Others like to do half-days the first few weeks, leaving the afternoons a bit freer and summer-like. Still others only focus on the two core subjects—math and language—during the first month of school and add in all the rest by month two.

Baptism by fire is a sure way to make anyone burn pretty hot. Launching the year at full-throttle on Day 1 will leave your entire family feeling overwhelmed, especially your strong-willed child. Soft-opening your year can be the grace he needs to homeschool well.

Create White Space

Even the friendliest of sibling relationships can turn sour when kids are packed like sardines together for large chunks of time each day. They, like all of us, crave a little elbow room and white space. Jesus acknowledged this very real need even in Himself. When He and the disciples were being pressed upon on all sides by a large crowd, he said, "Let's go off by ourselves to a quiet place and rest awhile" (Mark 6:31 NLT). At His bidding, they boarded a boat and went away to a place of solitude.

I'm a natural extrovert, but even I need a bit of alone time each day to refresh, regroup, and renew. How much more do my children who are just learning proper social skills and who spend nearly every waking minute together in a very small house need a bit of separation? I've learned through experience that homeschool relationships work best when I acknowledge my kids' desire for personal space and time.

When I find that sibling relationships are starting to get kind of spicy, I pull out our Quiet Basket—a large basket stuffed with interesting library books, puzzles, one-person games, and simple handwork. I instruct everyone to pick two items from the basket, find a relaxing spot somewhere in the house away from others, and sit quietly with focused attention on the two basket items for an allotted amount of time, usually twenty to thirty minutes. No one may get up or talk but must sit sedately working on the quiet activities of his choice.

Although these rules might seem rather rigid, there is hidden freedom in a fence. It allows any upset child a chance to calm down and gives all the others a bit of a respite from drama. As an added bonus, the time allows each of my kids to work on passions they might not otherwise have time for in a busy school day. By the end of the quiet time, they are all itching for time together again because they've had a chance to decompress and exhale away from one another.

Encourage Personal Responsibility

What looks like irresponsible behavior can sometimes just be childish immaturity that hasn't been ironed out yet. It's not uncommon for my wild one to tornado through his school day leaving piles of pencils, books, and project supplies in his wake. His immaturity and short attention span will improve eventually. But until then, I'm doing my best to encourage personal responsibility by making the mess more manageable for him.

At the beginning of each school year, I outfit all of my kids with color-coded school supplies, everything from pencils to pencil cases, spiral notebooks to scissors. Everyone's assigned a different color and all of their supplies reflect that. Then when I find something out of place or lying around, I know exactly whose it is and who needs to be prodded to put it back into place. Ownership and responsibility are built into the system, making it impossible for my wild one to blame-shift.

Most people believe that conflict and sibling rivalry are to be avoided. But it's in the conflict that basic heart issues and differences are brought to the surface and can be dealt with accordingly. Without the conflict, the sin issues fester and multiply. Sending your strong-willed child to public school might solve the struggles of the moment. It's obviously easier to put duct tape on brokenness than to actually fix it. But while duct tape solves a problem in the short term, it eventually wears away, revealing something even worse underneath. It's much better to face the struggles of a difficult child now in the greenhouse safety of your home than to ignore the problem and allow destructive behavior to grow unchecked just below the surface.

Foster Togetherness

Sometimes the struggle doesn't grow out of *different* but out of *same*. Like two similar magnetic poles, members of a home can be so similar that they end up spending most of the day repelling one another instead of drawing toward each other, adding unnecessary tension to the homeschool day. Such was the case with my daughter and me.

The summer before I started homeschooling, I nearly talked myself out of it. The preschool years had been delightful because we were a part of a budding group of young families all hoping to start homeschooling together the following year. There were four other girls in the bunch that were all near my daughter's age. I envisioned years of vibrant, growing friendships for my social butterfly. Like me, she had a large personality. But also like me, she could at times be a bit hot-headed and combative. A learning cooperative filled with other assertive voices besides my own would be a welcome force of influence on her developing character, I thought.

And then summer came, and my plan quickly collapsed. One by one, each of those families withdrew from the co-op. One moved out of state, another decided not to homeschool after all, and still another realized that a twice-a-month co-op would be too much of a strain on their schedule. Only one other family remained committed to the group, a family with two boys and one young girl still in training pants. Needless to say, my daughter and I were more than disappointed.

I began to panic. How in the world could I homeschool my just-like-me child without the friendships of other mother-daughter duos? We'd surely butt heads and spend most of our days in emotional gridlock. She needed girlfriends and other motherly influences in her life, didn't she? The writing on the wall was clear: homeschooling her would be a huge mistake. We'd no doubt spend our days pushing against one another, and that's not what I wanted for our relationship. But just when I was ready to secede and enroll her in the local school, God brought a veteran homeschool mom my way to calm my fears. With proven faith, she said, "If God has removed outside friendships from Maddie's homeschool experience and has left only you in their place, maybe He wants to give your relationship enough room to grow."

Reluctantly, even with the looming threat of loneliness (hers and mine), I agreed to obey the clear call to homeschool that I couldn't seem to shake. I wish I could tell you our first year was easy. It wasn't. I struggled with a lot of mom guilt because I felt that by choosing to homeschool, I was sentencing my daughter to a life without friends. In an effort to overcompensate, I began investing large amounts of time doing girly things with her. We had tea parties, played dress-up, read American Girl books, and co-hosted numerous get-togethers for girls of all ages in our community.

By year two, I began to see what God had planned in removing those four girlfriends and their families from our co-op the previous summer. He used solitude to bind her heart with mine. We were no longer butting heads and verbally arm wrestling through the day. Our relationship was strengthened, not because of a "perfect" homeschool plan, but in spite of an imperfect one. By year three, our co-op had grown to include not *one* additional girl my daughter's age, but *four*. In His timing, God waited to provide friends so that she and I could grow in grace together first.

> If God has called you to homeschool one of *those* kids, you can be sure He has a purpose for it.

I realize that not every scenario will tie up in such a neat little bow like ours did. Despite your best efforts, your days might still end up feeling like a clash of the Titans. But, as that wise woman reminded me all those years ago, if God has called you to homeschool one of *those* kids, you can be sure He has a purpose for it. Trust His plan and His transforming work in your life and in the life of your wild one. Know that there is something about homeschooling that He'll use to perfect both of you.

6

Struggling to Teach a Struggler

My homeschool is pretty mediocre. We have some great days—ones that look like the picturesque scenes of a Norman Rockwell painting. These idyllic days are almost otherworldly with my cherub-faced children gathered around close, all eager, attentive, and obedient. But then there are other days when regret marks our time together—days when learning doesn't come easily, when my kids don't give their best and when I don't give mine. Most days land somewhere in the middle, though. They're average. Run-of-the-mill, you might say. And that's as it should be.

It's important to be grateful for the *commonplace* of those days so that I don't get too discouraged on the days when things slide well below the midline, when tempers flare and tears fall. Admittedly, most of the time our struggles are character-related—when I've allowed habits to slip or ignored small offenses until everyone is fragile and ready to crack. But there are days when the battle has nothing to do with our bad attitudes, but everything to do with a child's struggle to learn or my struggle to teach. This is especially true for one of my sons, who has a learning disability.

To be honest, for a long while leading up to his kindergarten year, I wasn't sure if I could teach *this* child. I envisioned all my days ending like the last scene of a Greek tragedy, with me dragging myself away from the school table like the walking wounded. I was convinced there was no other path for him but the public school, with their special education inclusion plans. But when I was willing to get honest with myself, I knew deep in my bones that in passing my son's struggle off on someone else, I'd be obeying a gospel of convenience. I would be ignoring the work God was calling me to do.

Maybe you have a struggling learner too. Maybe your child seems grade levels behind his peers, doesn't understand, or still can't read. If you're anything like me, you've taken full ownership of the struggle. You wear it like a badge of shame—an ugly cloak that veils all the successes of your day, as if it's all your fault, as if you have done or haven't done something and have crippled your child's ability to ever get things right. You tell yourself that a "real" teacher would know how to do it better.

What you don't know, or perhaps what you may need to be reminded of, is that a "struggle" shows that you are doing something right. *Struggle* is a verb. It implies action; effort; giving it all you've got. If you are teaching a struggling learner, it means that you are, *right now,* developing a learner. You're not sitting idly by or watching from the sidelines. You're not growing comfortable with *good enough.* You've gathered all your pluck and moxie and are moving forward, helping him do the same.

Recently I was chatting with some other homeschool moms. We were all sharing our fears about our struggling readers. Did you catch that? We were *all* sharing. As in, we all have a struggling one. A common theme poured out. We all had a desire to unlock the mystery of words for our kids, to see the black-and-white text bring forth the color of a well-written story.

As I sat there with these ladies reflecting on our struggling ones caught somewhere between *I can't* and *I can,* I reminded them of one simple truth I've learned after teaching dozens and dozens and dozens of kids to read: they will all eventually be readers.

In the same way some toddlers potty-train overnight while others take months and even years, readers blossom in their own good time. I don't know of a single adult of sound mind and body who still wears training pants. Looking back at any when-will-this-child-ever-have-an-accident-free-day thoughts I may have had at one time, I have to roll my eyes. Did I really think I would still be diapering an eighteen-year-old? It sounds silly in hindsight, but I think there were moments when I had stamped *incontinence* as fact over my child's future.

Here are the brass tacks about potty-training: almost all kids get it eventually. That outcome applies to learning as well. Allow me to let you in on a little secret that the "real" teachers don't want you to know: they have struggling readers too.

When I was in the classroom, especially that one lovely year when I stared straight into a sea of six-year-old faces all anxiously awaiting their turn to cross the great divide between those who *can't* read and those who *can*, I did everything I could to forge readers. Everything. For most of my students, reading was the natural next step of their education. Words came easily for these ones. But, for others—a select few—they did not. It was a struggle, for them and for me.

You see, even if your child had one of those "real" teachers teaching him to read, he would probably still struggle. Why? Because God has given us all different strengths and weaknesses. Just as I cannot necessarily take the credit for my son's ability to paint like a budding Picasso, I also can't take the blame for his slow-and-steady start to reading. It was how he was created.

Those little doe-eyed six-year-olds of the "lovely year" have all grown up. In fact, many of them are married now with little ones of their own. (Yep, I'm *that* old. But let's not dwell on it.) And all those grown-up kids can read—every last one of them.

It's easy to think that all the difficulties of homeschool stem from schooling at home. They don't. The blunt fact is that often struggles like reading are actually amplified in the public school.

In the unavoidable caste system of a traditional classroom, artistic kids often get lost in the fray, advanced kids tend to misbehave out of boredom, and struggling readers get further and further behind. No matter what academic hardship your struggling one faces, know this: he would still face this same hurdle with the "other" guys.

So, momma with the struggling learner, let me lift your trembling chin and remind you that your struggling one *will* learn. Just keep struggling with him. Education is not a sprint, it's a marathon. Just keep moving forward.

> Education is not a sprint, it's a marathon. Just keep moving forward.

Please know my heart in this: I don't want to minimize your child's struggle. It's quite possible he suffers from dyslexia or another learning disability. This was the case for my struggling one, who at the age of six began showing signs of an irreversible nervous system disorder. This was confirmed a few years later, bringing a mixed bag of feelings ranging from relief to helplessness. His condition has made learning to read painstaking. But with time and much effort, he's doing it. He's reading. He's learning.

If you feel like your child's academic struggles are more than just the natural delays of self-paced learning, I'd highly recommend seeking professional help through private psychological and neurological testing facilities. Early diagnosis can help give your child tangible tools to set him on the path to success. It *is* possible to homeschool any child, even the ones who struggle greatly. In fact, I'll venture to say that in my experience of teaching struggling ones in the classroom and teaching my own son here at home, homeschooling affords not only a more realistic Independent Educational Plan (IEP), but also a gentler one because it can better accommodate for the emotional and social struggles that often accompany learning disabilities.

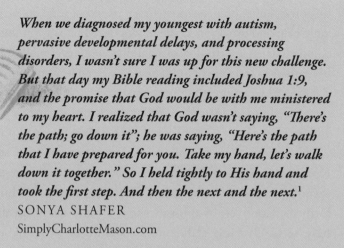

When we diagnosed my youngest with autism, pervasive developmental delays, and processing disorders, I wasn't sure I was up for this new challenge. But that day my Bible reading included Joshua 1:9, and the promise that God would be with me ministered to my heart. I realized that God wasn't saying, "There's the path; go down it"; he was saying, "Here's the path that I have prepared for you. Take my hand, let's walk down it together." So I held tightly to His hand and took the first step. And then the next and the next.[1]
SONYA SHAFER
SimplyCharlotteMason.com

That said, this is not a teacher's manual or a homeschooling how-to book, and I'm not a neurological expert. I'll not waste your time or mine giving you resources and opinions I have no business doling out. I'll only give you this one bottom-line: if you're homeschooling a struggling learner, you'll have to be more intentional than most to find ways of teaching from a place of abundance rather than scarcity, or you'll be worn slap-out from trying too hard. We'll talk more about self-preservation later. But for now, here are a few tips that might help you swallow down every little academic success in big thankful gulps.

Set Up Remembrance Stones

You and I are naturally forgetful. We're frail and fallen people who get too easily distracted by the problems of the present, forgetting about the successes of the past. Like the Israelites of old, we struggle to remember God's faithfulness to us and to our kids. We lose sight of all the Jordan Rivers He's parted and lions' mouths He's held shut on our behalf.

We, like the wandering ones of Joshua chapter 4, need to set up some remembrance stones to act as visual markers of God's daily help and provision in the school day. That way on the difficult days when it seems like our children won't ever move forward in math or in learning phonics blends, we can look at our memorial list and be reminded of how far they have come—how much they have learned. Instead of feeling stuck and stagnate, our kids will see all the growth that took place between then and now.

Here's how to stack a pile of academic remembrance stones. Keep a running list of what you know for sure. At the end of each day, spend a few moments recording what your child has learned. Better yet, have him write it all down. His list doesn't have to be anything elaborate; a sentence or two will suffice. Encourage him to think back through the day and write down anything and everything that he learned that day. His list might look something like this: *I learned to multiply by three today. A group of owls together is called a parliament.*

Naming the small wins will help you both to own them. One little victory doesn't seem like much, but when it's stacked on top of other small things, it will. Every line item on the list will not necessarily hold the same weight as everything else. But seeing dozens of learned skills next to one or two unmastered goals will put learning into perspective. As an added bonus, the next time the child gets drilled about what he's learning by an inappropriately curious cashier at the grocery store, he won't have to stare blankly into the abyss. He'll have a few thoughts at-the-ready with which to share because he'll have already determined what he knows for sure.

A list of remembrance will act like an altar of stones so that "all the peoples of the earth [or at least the ones in your home] might know that the hand of the Lord is powerful" (Josh. 4:24 NIV). God was faithful in today's school assignments and will be just as faithful in tomorrow's.

Document Improvement through Recorded Reading

I have a large wooden plank lining one of the walls in my main floor hallway. It stretches from floor to ceiling and is painted to look like a giant ruler. While that simple board adds a certain whimsy to the otherwise empty hall, its purpose for hanging there is quite practical. It's a growth chart. Over the years, I've scratched names, dates, and height marks all along its left side to mark the physical growth of each of my kids. Funny thing is, every year as I line my kids up against the wall and press their heads to the plank, I'm always shocked to see just how much they've grown in one year's time. From day to day, I obviously know that they are growing. My increasing grocery bill and their shrinking pant legs are proof of that. But growth happens slowly and often goes unnoticed when I'm not taking the time to look for it. The growth chart makes it easier to see the difference.

Just as you can miss the physical growth of kids, you can also miss their academic growth if you're not looking for it and marking it down. This is especially true if the largest academic hurdle is in the area of reading. Part of the apprehension of reading for a struggling learner is that he can't see steady, daily progression of improvement. What he read yesterday seemed hard. What he is reading today seems harder. And, in his mind, what he will read tomorrow will probably be the hardest of all.

Chances are, in the thick of struggle, his view of reading has grown a bit myopic. He can't see how far he's come because he fails to remember that the sounds and words he learned to read at the beginning of the year seemed hard because they were hard *then*. By the end of the year, those same sounds are quite easy for him to read because he's had a year's worth of practice at them. He doesn't always recognize the graduated incline of his reading skills because, like physical growth, academic growth happens slowly over time. What he needs is a growth chart to show the dramatic difference.

I'd encourage you to use your smartphone or another digital

device to record your child's progress so that you don't unintentionally miss it. These recordings won't be used to keep score or to create "proof" for the state or nosy neighbor. They will only ever be heard or seen by you and by him. They will act as a growth chart.

Start by recording your child reading a selection from the book he currently finds most difficult. Set this recording aside and continue with reading lessons as usual for a few weeks. Then after he has learned and practiced and learned some more, revisit that very same book. Re-record him reading the same passages as before, and then compare the two recordings. Continue to re-record every few months. Just be sure to record him reading the exact same book or selection every time. Barring some phonics-related catastrophe, he will probably improve throughout the year and the growth will be obvious. The readings will sound smoother and smoother, providing him with tangible proof that his reading has improved. The success will feel like a desperate breath to a phonemic asthmatic.

Go Beyond Reading, 'Riting, and 'Rithmetic

Let's do a little truth-telling here, shall we? It's just the two of us, and this is a safe space. There is a trend in homeschooling circles for moms to *go easy* on themselves in order to avoid burnout. There are whole books dedicated to the idea of back-to-basics learning, encouraging all of us to only do the three *R*'s of reading, 'riting, and 'rithmetic. The theory being that if we go light on ourselves, our school days will be simpler; we'll avoid stress; and we'll enjoy the journey so much better. And while that's true in some cases and on certain days, whether we want to admit it or not, light learning often has the opposite effect in homes of struggling ones like ours.

The ho-hum nature of math and language can easily create an uninspiring school year. Traditional subjects have a tendency to divide kids into two camps—those who are academic and those who are not. The children who struggle with worksheets and the two-dimensional learning style of textbooks are stamped as "dumb" or "slow," regardless of their talent, creativity, leadership skills, or character.

In contrast with the three *R*'s, nontraditional, passion-driven extras like art, nature study, music, or computer coding give a struggling learner a chance to feel capable and valued. Don't get me wrong, I'm not advocating that you squeeze a three-ring-circus into your school day or allow your kids to participate in every single available extra-curricular. I'm merely suggesting that you determine which "extra" really inspires and reassures your struggling child and make *that* the fourth *R* on your to-do list. Everyone deserves to feel the lift of success, especially those kids who spend most of the day feeling below the bar.

> Determine which "extra" really inspires and reassures your struggling child.

Stop Dangling Carrots

For whatever reason, adults think that prizes, sticker charts, and cheap plastic incentives motivate children. While these types of "carrots" certainly make magic happen for all of one minute, they actually do the very opposite in the long haul. Will a struggling learner work really quickly and with a smile at the promise of candy? You bet. Won't we all? We're a society driven by gold stars. I'd do just about anything for mint-flavored Oreos. But I also have no control over myself when I eat them. They're my kryptonite. (Don't tell my kids. That could be a bit problematic.) But what about tomorrow when the cookie jar is empty or the sticker chart is filled up? What happens to a child's drive and motivation then? It plummets, and he naturally develops a "What's in it for me?" attitude. The shelf-life of dangled carrots is minimal, at best. And like most out-of-date foodstuffs, they turn sour quickly, growing an unwelcome demand for more dangling carrots.

Education doesn't have to be fun, even for struggling ones. Education should be engaging. It should propel a child toward curiosity and wonder. *Fun* falls too short. Learning should be a deeper pursuit. Granted, every lesson and concept isn't going to be awe-inspiring. Whether he likes it or not, your child will someday need to learn to find the lowest common denominator or to start a sentence with a capital letter. There are many uninteresting but important skills that will require him to just lean in and persevere. There are always lessons that can be learned by just doing the next mundane thing. But, trust me, artificial leverage won't help. Nothing will ruin your homeschool quite like the cheap, the vain, or the contrived.

> Education doesn't have to be fun. Education should be engaging. It should propel a child toward curiosity and wonder. *Fun* falls too short. Learning should be a deeper pursuit.

A "fun" home education is one in which a mother has to wildly wave Muppet hands in order to get anyone's attention. A "fun" education puts the pressure on her to produce just the right environment. A "fun" education breeds a lazy learner who never explores, creates, or dives deep because he never has to. Information is handed to him on a glittering silver platter.

A true education is one in which a child personally invests, one that he is passionate about, one that inspires, not requires, him to learn. A child who is fully engaged doesn't need Muppet hands or made-up incentives. He owns his own learning. It's about *him* and *his* effort. It's not about *you* and *yours*. So can we all just stop it with the plastic and sugar-coated propaganda?

Despite my initial fears, my struggling learner has grown into a well-rounded, highly inquisitive young man. He still finds it difficult at times to keep pace with the rigidity of a traditional program, but every hard-won victory pushes him further in his desire to learn more. Homeschooling has been the perfect fit for him because it's allowed for a tailor-made education.

I've no doubt that these years of persistence will serve him well when he's faced with the challenges of adulthood. We've both homeschooled long enough to trust the journey. He's learned not to topple at the first sign of trouble. And I've learned that struggle-filled days, weeks, or even months don't derail an education. As long as my children can each get forward motion bit-by-bit, it will all add up. There will still be fruit.

7

Little People and Big Messes

I f you're knee-deep in toddler tenacity right now, you're probably blurry-eyed and running on coffee fumes. Glory be. You may feel like it's difficult enough just to occupy your small people, better yet enjoy them. But it doesn't have to be an either/or equation. You can have both—pinky swear.

Need I remind you, the toddler years are only temporary? Isn't that liberating? I know that when you're in the thick of the toddler rodeo show it seems like an eternity. Toddler years are like dog years: one feels like seven. But the good thing is, like puppies, toddlers grow and mature really quickly. They aren't the same people today that they were last week. By the end of the school year, you'll have a completely different child on your hands.

I'm not trying to massage the truth here. I get it. I've faced your same frustration. I've had days when the heavy work of homeschooling a billion tiny people made me feel defeated by lap one. I've experienced entire weeks of baby wrangling that should have come with hard hats and hazard signs. *Falling rocks. Bridge is out.* I've white-knuckled more than my share of moments. To call me patient and tender during that entire season would be rather generous. *Overwhelm* was riding shotgun with me through most of it. But I made it. We all made it because babies don't stay babies for very long.

All that to say, if you feel suffocated by unnecessary guilt because you are only getting to the essentials each day and wondering if homeschooling with a tot is even sustainable, be encouraged by brevity. Can your older kids survive one month? Six months? A year without doing those fancy art projects you have your heart set on, making a history diorama for each era you study, creating those one-of-a-kind lapbooks? Of course they can. You just have to shelf all those extras for a season. Listen, you cannot do more today than today allows. You cannot do more than God has for you.

> You cannot do more today than today allows. You cannot do more than God has for you.

I've always imagined that homeschooling with a tot must be kind of like the feeling you'd get if you were running with the bulls—and then someone handed you a toddler! Perhaps the comparison sounds a bit casually offensive. But from this side of the bleachers, both scenarios look about the same to me. If you're currently trying to keep your head low in order to weather the toddler storm, it probably sounds accurate to you too.

But what if we all stopped looking at toddlers as sand in the gears, as little interruptions to our daily lessons? What if we realized that sometimes the toddler *is* the lesson?

Mama of littles, what if your older children could see you handle the tears and frustration of a toddler with love and empathy? What if they could see you clean up *another* mess with grace and forgiveness? How would that change the landscape of your days? What if how you handle the inconvenience and interruption of a toddler *is* the lesson, perhaps the only lesson, that your children learn in their homeschool this year? Would that be a failure?

Remember, sometimes your days will be *home*school and sometimes they will be home*school*. That balance between the two is a delicate one, to be sure. In reality, your greatest virtue as a homeschool mother of tots will be your ability to live in the tension between them both.

You were called to the job of motherhood long before you began homeschooling. Your older kids have the rest of their lives to learn division facts and participial phrases, but your toddler will only be little for a short time. In the busyness of the school day, don't just "occupy" your smallest gifts, enjoy them, invest in them, delight in them.

> *Time is short, and children grow quickly. Although we do not know how much time we will have, we do have today, and we can make these our top priorities: character, knowledge, skills. . . . Mark Twain said, "I have never let my schooling interfere with my education." What may have been humor then is deep wisdom for us now; we must never let our concept of what "school" should be eclipse the education our children truly need.*[1]
>
> ANDREW PUDEWA
> founder and director of The Institute for Excellence in Writing

Looking back, when I was in the thick of it all, I'll have to admit I didn't really need another tip, trick, or strategy. What I craved was for someone to *see me*—for someone to understand and acknowledge how very hard it really was to homeschool with tots. I wasn't looking for a banner or a trophy or a parade in my honor. Nope. I never wanted anything quite that fancy.

I just needed a little solidarity from someone who had walked this same difficult road. I needed someone to show me the sacred in the mundane and remind me that there were miracles to be found in all the monotony of caring for small people.

Well, Tired Mama, God sees you. He is *El Roi*, the God Who Sees, after all. He sees you rushing into the co-op meeting, carrying a baby and a diaper bag in your arms while dragging a crying toddler behind you. He sees the look of embarrassment and exasperation you try to hide behind a well-rehearsed smile. He sees you heave a sigh as you sit on the bench nursing your baby during a field trip while silently praying your toddler doesn't wander out of reach. He sees that under your squared shoulders and resolute determination, you are tired. You are weary. You are worn thin.

God sees you spinning all those plates. He sees you holding your breath hoping they don't all come crashing down. He sees you carrying around the weight of the elusive "perfect" homeschool day.

God sees you, and I see you too. I see you because, as I mentioned, I was you. In the not-so-distant past, I was the homeschool mom with four littles under the age of five. I had one moving from kindergarten to first grade, and I desperately wanted to be the "good" homeschool mom for her sake—to provide her with those memorable *firsts* that all the other homeschool moms talked about.

I wanted to plan the unit studies and make the lapbooks. I wanted to take the field trips and create the art projects. I wanted to do all the worthwhile things that make learning worthwhile. But I couldn't. I was outnumbered—surrounded by little people and big messes.

Admittedly, I didn't do everything right back then. My shoulda-coulda-wouldas stack up pretty high. But there were a few things I did do that seemed to help hold back the hot flames of the tot years. Here are a few ideas that worked for me. Don't you dare look at anything on this list as a *have to*. That will only add more weight to your already hard-to-lift days. Just put them in the *maybe* pile, and try only the ones that make good sense to you.

Create a Tot School

September, with its new books, clothes, and school supplies, can often feel like Christmas to kids. But just imagine if you had to see everyone around you enjoy "Christmas" while you only got to watch from the sidelines. You'd feel a bit out of the circle, wouldn't you? Oftentimes, this is how the beginning of the school year seems to the three-and-under crowd. Your tot watches everyone receive shiny new stuff while he sits empty-handed.

Although a toddler may not need a pencil box or fresh coloring supplies, he'd probably be thrilled to get them alongside everyone else. In the long run, filling a school box with simple items like new puzzles, lace-n-trace cards, preschool board games, and picture books would be a small price to pay for helping to make your tot feel welcome in your school.

Full disclosure, however: It's gonna take more than a box of crayons to keep a toddler tended for the long haul. New school supplies will entertain a two-year-old for all of one minute. *Crazy* will surely find you if you don't start the school year with a more elaborate plan. Press hard into this grim reality, mark it down, and memorize it: If *you* don't have a plan, your *toddler* sure will, and you'll spend most of the school year cleaning up the collateral damage.

Planning a constructive day will require some calculated scheduling. You'll have to pencil in specific times of the day when you or your older children can spend one-on-one time with your babies or tots. Chances are, you already schedule the time you spend with your big kids and loosely plan out their school assignments and activities. You need to start doing that same kind of deliberate planning for your tot. This will ensure that you actually do it and will prevent you from just passing him all of your leftover energy. It will make your preschooler feel important and that he matters too. Having a purposeful plan for your tot will also remind the other children that just as you don't like to be interrupted during a math lesson, you don't want to be interrupted while building blocks or finger painting. Planning will give the tot-time gravity.

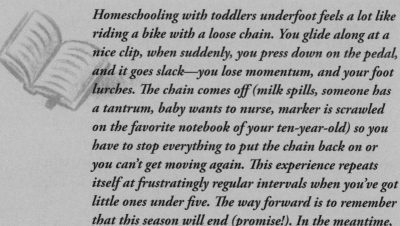

Homeschooling with toddlers underfoot feels a lot like riding a bike with a loose chain. You glide along at a nice clip, when suddenly, you press down on the pedal, and it goes slack—you lose momentum, and your foot lurches. The chain comes off (milk spills, someone has a tantrum, baby wants to nurse, marker is scrawled on the favorite notebook of your ten-year-old) so you have to stop everything to put the chain back on or you can't get moving again. This experience repeats itself at frustratingly regular intervals when you've got little ones under five. The way forward is to remember that this season will end (promise!). In the meantime, use nontraditional school hours to work with older kids: evenings, when the other parent is home; Sunday afternoons away from home; during the toddler's nap. Remember: your older kids are still learning, even if interrupted. On truly awful days, abandon it all and head to the park![2]

JULIE BOGART
creator of Brave Writer, and author of *The Brave Learner*

When mapping out how best to spend quality pockets of time with your tot, start with the first few minutes of the school day. Most of the time, the mischief of a toddler stems from a desperate plea for attention. By giving the first and best part of each school day to your little one, you will fill his love tank. Afterward, he'll probably be more than ready to toddle off for independent play, having been awarded your undivided attention right off the top. At the beginning of the school year, teach your older kids to self-launch one activity at the start of each day in order that you can dedicate the first fifteen minutes to spending intentional one-on-one time with your tot.

Obviously, your littlest one will need more mothering than just a few minutes in the morning. But before you start manipulating your days like a contortionist, stand down and recognize your limitations. Despite your good intentions, it's not going to be possible for you as a homeschool mom to cuddle your baby or toddler all day *and* teach your other children *and* keep up with all that a home demands *and* play doting wife to your husband—all at the same time. Spoiler alert: You are only one person with a finite ability to do one thing at a time.

But remember *home*school means everyone in the home plays a special part in the grand plan. If you have older kids, then you have extra pairs of hands that are probably more than willing to take their turn doing puzzles, reading books, stacking blocks, or just cuddling on the couch with your smallest people.

Break the day into ten- or fifteen-minute increments and assign each of your older kids to a rotation of playing "teacher" to your babies and tots during school hours. Be sure to emphasize the fact that this time is for the tot, not the older child. The play should always be something that the baby or tot wants to do. Don't forget to include yourself in the cycle. This will not only save your sanity, but will also help to form lasting sibling relationships, cultivate a sense of responsibility in your older kids, and provide even kids as young as five or six a chance to serve others right in their own home.

> Remember *home*school means everyone in the home plays a special part in the grand plan.

In spending time with your younger ones, your big kids will model habits and skills to their younger siblings. When your toddler is finally old enough to join the more official parts of your homeschool, you won't have to teach him the basic rituals and routines of your day because he'll have been gradually taught by the example of his brothers and sisters during Tot School.

As you are creating your daily plan, remember to write it in pencil. When dealing with toddlers who change course at lightning speed, even the best-laid plans only have about a three-month's expiration date, if that. So be willing and ready to tweak your schedule often.

Handwork for Toddlers

Once you've outlined a tentative plan, brainstorm some "school" activities that you think will occupy your tot in a pinch. Make a master list of every tot game and age-appropriate activity that you have around the house so that during a frenzied school day, you won't have to expend unnecessary brain power trying to think of something for your little one to do. A master list will make Tot School an unfold-and-inflate situation. You and your older kids will be able to consult the list and decide in an instant what to pull out or set up.

Just so we're clear, "Tot School" is not really school. You'll just call it that for the sake of your little one who wants it to feel "official." Babies and toddlers don't need rigid workbooks and flashcards. They need play.

Don't bother scanning Pinterest for elaborate preschool projects, often called Busy Bags. Trust me, that's a fool's errand that will leave you both emotionally and financially bankrupt. You'll spend hours of time and gobs of money creating picture-worthy Busy Bags only to later realize that your kid would rather just play with the box you've packed them all in instead.

That's why my secret sauce during those tot years was handwork. Using twiddly bits that I had just lying around my house, I created dozens of playful diversions for my curious tot to do during the homeschool day.

Here's a carefully curated list of supplies for my best no-fuss "Tot School" handwork activities. Most of these won't just occupy your tot, they will also develop the fine motor and cognitive thinking skills he'll need for writing and reading someday. Pick a few you think will be the most appealing and engaging for your little one, place the necessary items for each one in a plastic zipper bag or storage tub, and stash them all away in a closet with your master list of activities. When it's time for Tot School, encourage your child to undertake handwork alongside you or a responsible older sibling.

Handwork for 1- to 2-year-olds
- Put together a chunky wooden puzzle.
- Create a disappearing picture using a small amount of water in a shallow bowl, a paintbrush, and a piece of colored construction paper.
- Make a cloud picture by gluing cotton balls onto dots of glue that have been dolloped onto a piece of blue construction paper.
- "Cook" with discarded plastic food containers and measuring spoons in a sink with a slow drip of water.
- Draw chalk pictures using sidewalk chalk on big pieces of newsprint or construction paper.
- Drop playing cards one-at-a-time into a card-sized slit in the lid of an empty, clean oatmeal bucket. Once all the cards have been dropped, empty the container, and begin dropping the cards again.
- Push and pull ribbon or fabric scraps into the top of a discarded, clean baby-wipe box.
- Color-rub with the length-side of an unwrapped crayon and a piece of paper that's been placed on top of a sheet of sandpaper or the sand-papery side of a wooden puzzle.

Handwork for 2- to 3-year-olds

- Complete any of the activities previously listed.
- Paint with water using a paintbrush and a small amount of water in an empty bathtub or on a porch.
- Put magnets/magnet dolls on a small metal baking sheet to create a scene.
- *"Bake"* cookies with homemade or store-bought play dough, a rolling pin, and cookie cutters.
- Shoot disposable drinking straw "spears" through the holes of an upside-down laundry basket.
- Build a rocket ship, house, or grocery store out of a large appliance box.
- Finger paint without a mess. Pour a few dollops of washable paint onto a piece of art paper; place the paper inside a zipper bag; use packing tape to reinforce all the edges; and lay the bag paint-side up onto a workspace. Rub fingers across the sealed bag to create pictures.
- "Sew" with lace-and-trace card sets.
- Match colored or patterned socks.
- String looped cereal through lengths of yarn.
- Play "car wash" using plastic or metal toy cars, a scrub brush, a washrag, a washtub filled with a small amount of water, and a towel.
- Give a set of plastic animals a bath using a scrub brush, a washrag, a washtub filled with a small amount of water, and a towel.
- Race toy cars through an empty wrapping-paper tube.
- Sort toy cars by color onto construction paper "parking spots."
- Squish a sensory bag made from a zipper bag filled with dollar-store hair gel, wiggly eyes, glitter, and small trinkets. Reinforce the edges with packing tape, place the bag on a workspace, and use fingers to squish the contents.

- Draw erasable pictures with fingers onto a tray that has been sprinkled with cornmeal or baking flour.
- Clip and unclip clothespins onto the lip of a discarded plastic food container.

Handwork for 3- to 4-year-olds

- Complete any of the activities previously listed.
- Sort colored milk caps, craft pompoms, building bricks, or other small items by size, shape, or color in the cups of a muffin tin.
- Create a sticker picture using stickers or old address labels.
- Pour and dump dried beans or rice into plastic containers of various sizes using measuring cups, spoons, and funnels.
- Tear or use safety scissors to cut scraps of paper or junk mail.
- String chunky wooden beads onto lengths of yarn to create color patterns.
- Design a collage or simple mosaic using scraps of paper, leaves, or fabric swatches. Use tape to adhere a sheet of contact paper sticky-side up onto a workspace. Arrange the scraps to form a pattern or picture on the contact paper.
- Excavate small toys out of a block of ice. Place small items in a plastic container, fill the remaining space of the container with water, and freeze overnight. The next day, remove the frozen puck from the container and place in an empty wash tub. Fill a small cup with warm water, and slowly pour the water onto the frozen puck, revealing the toys inside.
- Make a matching game out of paint chip samples and clothespins. Write a number, upper-case letter, or a swatch of color onto the end of a clothespin. Write a corresponding number of dots, lower-case letter, or color word onto a paint chip. Clip the clothespin onto the appropriate paint chip.
- Dig for buried treasure in a sandbox or bin. Bury coins or

small toys in the sand and then use a spoon to dig them out.

- Play "grocery store" using empty food boxes and containers, an inexpensive or broken calculator, and cloth or paper grocery bags.

- Create a stamp picture using rubber stamps, washable ink pads, and craft paper.

- Draw a mural on a window or glass door using washable markers.

- Paint a dot picture using washable Bingo daubers.

- Match magnetic numbers or letters inside the compartments of an egg carton that have each been labeled with the appropriate numbers or letters.

- Match small colored objects from around the house or from nature to the compartments of an egg carton that have each been painted different colors.

Handwork for 4- to 5-year-olds

- Complete any of the activities previously listed.

- Create a color-matching memory game using paint chip samples from a hardware store. You will need two paint chip samples of each color to play.

- Race small balls or marbles down a pool noodle that has been cut in half lengthwise.

- Play "bank" using pencils, small pads of paper, play money, old bank register booklets, and a calculator.

- Mix colors. Partially fill several clear cups with water. Place a different colored drop of food coloring into each cup and stir. Use a medicine dropper to suction the colored water from one cup to another and watch the colors change.

- Finger paint with shaving cream that's been sprayed onto a cookie sheet.

- Strap handfuls of rubber bands around a glass jar. Then unstrap them.

- Build and tinker with small objects like empty spools of thread, popsicle sticks, paper clips, gears from broken watches, a small flashlight, a magnifying glass, disposable safety glasses, etc. that have been placed inside an inexpensive toolbox or craft caddy.

- Pound golf tee "nails" into a cardboard box or a block of packing Styrofoam using a soft mallet purchased at the dollar store.

A Hindsight View

That living-on-two-hours-of-sleep-and-twelve-cups-of-coffee season of babies and toddlers is mostly a blur at this point. The one thing I can keenly remember about those days each time I see you drive up to the homeschool park day with a van crowded with car seats is how hard it was and how, at the time, I desperately wanted someone, anyone, to understand the hardness of it all.

So many days felt like one hot mess of chaos after another. I didn't have enough arms, enough eyes, enough time, enough energy for all those little ones. My shoulders just weren't wide enough to carry all of that—or so it seemed.

But I made it, and you will too. And what's more, you will look back on these days of my-homeschool-feels-like-a-blender-with-the-cap-off with fondness.

I know it doesn't seem like it now. Right now you are having trouble seeing past this very moment of deafening noise and constant motion. Right now you are just hoping to salvage each and every day. Right now you are trying to convince yourself *not* to huddle in the corner and eat all the chocolate. But, trust me. Fondness will find its way into your memories of these toddler years.

Recently, while looking through old photographs of those early homeschooling days, I was reminded of the beauty that can often only be seen through a rearview mirror. When I sifted through all those pictures, I didn't see the Sharpie marker that

suddenly found its way to my bedspread and curtains and carpet during art time one day. I didn't see the store display shelf
knocked over by a very curious toddler during a spontaneous
field trip. I didn't see the library book pages cut out by a little
boy who had just learned to use his scissors. I didn't see any of
the dumpster fire days. I just saw the smiling faces of kids learning and growing and loving each other. I saw a storehouse of
memories we had built together.

And my daughter? The one I was so worried I was failing because I couldn't seem to provide even one "normal" day for her?
She's in high school now. And I'm not overselling in the slightest
when I say she's kind and compassionate, smart and determined.
She learned patience all those years ago when her school work
couldn't always be done *this very moment*. She learned gentleness
when she had to help rock a crying little one. She learned forgiveness when she had to start a project all over again because
it got destroyed by a younger sibling. She learned independence
when she had to find the answer without my help.

Determined Homeschool Mom trying to do good by your
little one, you, too, will look back and see smiling faces. You,
too, will be able to enjoy the toddler years through the beauty
and wonder of hindsight. In the meantime, remember this: God
sees you. I see you.

8

One Crazy Day Away from Crisis

He stood there, tears brimming the corners of his eyes. He was only three and didn't quite understand. Golly, even at nearly thirty, I didn't fully comprehend it myself. We both just stared with gaping mouths at all the struggle, feeling helpless. No, not exactly helpless, for we certainly could have helped. But even with my limited experience, I knew our help would have hindered, probably even crippled any potential success. But how could I explain that to my son as he sat watching the jar in anguish, desperately wanting to reach out and end what seemed to him to be strife and suffering?

We were gathered around an old pickle jar, anxiously watching as a butterfly, our summertime science project, wrestled its way into the world. Its once protective chrysalis now seemed to be an anchor weighing it down. The butterfly writhed and wiggled, desperately trying to free its wings. It was a violent dance but one choreographed by a Creator who knows all the hidden and silent secrets of nature.

Surely it was only a matter of moments before the limp wings emerged from their captivating shell, but to us, it seemed like hours. The process looked painful and pointless. We could have easily just peeled the soft shell away from the butterfly, freeing him from the struggle. But we didn't.

"He needs to build his muscles," I said to my son, gently wiping away a tear that had escaped down his cheek. It was a simple explanation for what I knew to be true: there was a point to the struggle. It was God-designed. It's in the pushing and pulling that butterflies constrict their abdomens, allowing a yellowish blood called hemolymph to fill their wing veins. Without that transfer of blood, the abdomen would be too heavy and the wings would never be able to fully extend.[1]

Watching the struggle as a bystander was difficult. But I knew the struggle would help our butterfly grow into what it was supposed to be. If I took away the struggle, I'd also take away the flight.

It's the same way with homeschooling. You can't always opt out of the struggle for you or your child. Sometimes you have to sit in the discomfort of it for your own good and for theirs. More often than not, there's a *someday* point to the pain of right now.

You can't always opt out of the struggle for you or your child. Sometimes you have to sit in the discomfort of it for your own good and for theirs.

At the risk of pouring salt into a raw wound, I'm going to take a wild guess and assume you or your child are facing some kind of struggle that has become a burden on your attempt to homeschool. *Struggle* seems to be the common denominator of humanity. It's universal. Jesus put it this way, "In this world you will have trouble" (John 16:33 NIV). So whether you find yourself in a momentary calm or in the very center of a storm, one thing's for sure: difficulties are close within reach. *Struggle* is synonymous with this world.

You might be only one crisis away from crazy and can't see how you can keep school spinning any longer. But don't forget that Christ's best moments of teaching were wrapped in chaos too. In crowded homes, along the lakeshore, and even in the house of God, Jesus was familiar with messy living. He had to teach stubborn people who refused to listen. He fought to be heard above crying babies and noisy animals. The smell of dirty diapers was masked only by the pungent fog of rotting fish being washed ashore at His feet. He was surrounded by needy people pressing in on Him, clinging to Him. Sound familiar? He was faced with death, disease, and hopeless situations at every turn. Still, He taught. He used these very circumstances as life lessons. He used them to teach hard things in gentle ways.

It's easy to get upset at God for the struggles of this world— for the difficulties of your life, including homeschool. You're human. Doubt comes with the flesh. But aren't you so glad that you can't always figure out God's plans and His ways? I know I am. If I could somehow sleuth my way to all the answers, that would mean I could fit all of His plans and ways into my teeny-tiny brain. And quite frankly, I wouldn't want to serve a god that I, of all people, could figure out. I'm not always happy with unanswered questions, but I'm content with my ignorance. His ways are much higher than my understanding—and that is good.

I *love* homeschooling, but to be honest, sometimes I only *like* it for exactly 0 seconds. I remember one day not so long ago that I ended our school time feeling mentally wounded. The day was tough. I caught one boy in a tangled web of lies and had to walk him through repentance and restitution. I listened as another boy used up all his words on me until I thought my ears were going to bleed. My daughter had started a ministry project that required much more of my help than I was anticipating. And my laptop decided to boycott math. (I completely understood the boycott. As I've mentioned, I live in a constant state of animosity with numbers. But that day was not a great day for technology to malfunction, even for math.) I ended the afternoon feeling calloused and bruised. It would have been easy for me to second-guess my decision to homeschool when I wasn't seeing any fruit of that choice.

The Treasures in the Darkness

Sometimes, though, the dark days bring about the biggest blessings. Take a look at Isaiah 45:3, which reads, "I will give you the treasures of darkness and the hoards in secret places, that you may know that it is I, the LORD, the God of Israel, who call you by your name." It's often in the struggles that we find the best things of life. Birth from birth pains, freedom from war, gold medals from years of grueling work and self-denial.

> Sometimes the dark days bring about the biggest blessings.

I found treasures even on that dark day. God used my emotional poverty to reveal some untended places in my heart. He chiseled away at my impatience, selfishness, and pride to make me more like Him. Some days His shaping comes by way of a scalpel. That day it felt more like a chainsaw. (I'm a hard lump, to be sure.) But when all was said and done, I was one step closer to the completed me. I may have ended the day feeling mentally wounded, but I was also spiritually grateful.

My homeschool is not immune to struggle. It's seen more than its share of misery. Several years ago, my kids had to watch as I said goodbye to my dad, who died after a string of strokes. While in my grief I would have liked to stay in bed until the end of time, life had to go on. My homeschool still had to go on. Fortunately, it didn't need to happen with quite the same momentum as it usually did. In fact, it couldn't. I didn't have it in me. I had to forfeit some of my original plans and revamp others. Mostly I just put one foot in front of the other and kept

> *It's totally normal to question your ability to homeschool your kids. We want the best for our kids. Hard days and exhaustion can mess with the best of us and cause us to doubt. However, I trust that God will give me strength and wisdom as I homeschool my kids. I also remind myself that there is no teacher who will love my kids more and be more devoted to their success.*[2]
> KRISTI CLOVER
> coauthor of *Homeschool Basics* and host of the *Simply Joyful Podcast*

moving forward as well as I could.

Around that same time, another homeschooling mom who just happened to be one of my dearest friends had to bury her two-year-old son. The entirety of his life was spent in and out of hospitals, fighting for one more day. Through those difficult years, his older three siblings got a completely different education from the one their mom had planned. Their days were spent in waiting rooms, hospital hallways, and eventually hospice care. They lived lifetimes in those twenty-four months.

Illness, death, job loss, spousal abandonment—I've visited with homeschooling moms who have experienced any and all of these. Their homeschools have been laden with struggles of all kinds. And while their specific circumstances have varied, their survival instincts have all been the same. They all recognized their need to pare down and homeschool differently, at least for a while.

Delight Instead of Defeat

If you're in a similar season of struggle or chaos, don't be ashamed to undertake the bare minimum. Ask yourself, "If my kids only finish one subject today, what do I hope it will be?" Maybe at this point, the thought of completing even *one* whole lesson seems unrealistic. Pick a few specific skills within that subject to practice instead. In other words, if introducing long division today is not possible, just review regular division problems for a bit, then have your child rehearse his subtraction facts on his own. Both skills will eventually combine to form the foundation of long division, so you'll at least be greasing the wheel for the day when life returns to normal and you can do a complete math lesson again. Reviewing previously learned material is never a waste of time even if that's all that gets done in the day.

If you, like my friend, find yourself bouncing from this doctor's appointment to that consultation, create a mobile classroom by packing a school-on-the-go bag. Along with one or two essential subjects, pack a backpack with earbuds and audiobooks, educational board games, documentaries, historical biographies, age-appropriate current event magazines, and simple handwork projects like paint-by-number sets or needlepoint. All of these can easily be assigned and enjoyed in the car or in a waiting room. Most can be started, stopped, and picked up again at a later time.

A couple of years ago, when I found myself taking all five of my kids on day trips to the big city and back every few months for my daughter's cardiology appointments, I never mourned the loss of what I thought school was supposed to be or counted those irregular days in the casualty column. Instead, I chose to see them for what they really were: a chance to show my kids the treasures in the darkness and to teach through the real lessons of life.

That year for a nominal flat rate, I bought a reciprocating-admissions pass that granted my entire family entrance to dozens of museums, zoos, and historical sites around our state. Whenever we had to travel for a doctor's visit, I planned field trips before and after the appointment, bookending our day with out-of-the-box learning. Most of the time, we enjoyed academically heavy places like science centers and living history museums.

But sometimes we just enjoyed the everyday offerings of an urban area that we small-town folk rarely got to experience. Once we even went to an organic, international market to grab some snacks, wandered around the entire store, and counted the simple shopping trip as "school" because my kids had never been to a store like that before. It was a day filled with echocardiograms and delicious samples of ensaïmada. Without the struggle, we would have missed both.

This is not a call to just "buck up" or "get over it." My point is not to give you another formula to lay over your days or to dismiss the very real pain of them, but only to encourage you to relinquish your tight hold of homeschooling in the midst of your difficulty. In doing so, you'll begin to see *delight* instead of defeat. Might I encourage you to welcome a new approach to teaching, one that requires less from you? During this struggle-filled season, consider trying a more interest-led education through strewing or project-based learning. These methods are not just helpful during moments of crisis, but on normal homeschool days too (if those even exist!).

> Relinquish your tight hold of homeschooling in the midst of your difficulty. You'll begin to see *delight* instead of defeat.

Strewing, sometimes referred to as delight-directed learning, is organic school and uses a full spectrum of experiences to nurture curiosity. Similarly, project-based learning encourages a child to create, experiment, or build something in order to discover more about a particular topic. When the project is completed, a child presents it to an audience—in this case, his family or a group of friends.

Both of these methods are practically torn right from the pages of the children's classic *If You Give a Mouse a Cookie*, as they use a pre-existing interest or passion to lure a child into another interest or passion. One topic leads to the next, which leads to the next. Like a farmer strewing seeds in a field, all you have to do for both delight-directed and project-based learning is toss out a few ideas or lay out a few interesting items, welcome boredom, and watch as a child's natural curiosity begins to take over, growing new areas of interest.

Take Legos, for instance. Like most ten-year-old boys, my son is obsessed with them. Unless he's tasked with a particular school assignment or a chore, he can always be found in his bedroom buried under a work in progress. To be honest, if he could build himself a little colony of mini-figures, I think he'd declare himself king and start structuring the world's first plastic monarchy so he'd never have to leave his Lego corner again.

Now I could just let him continue to build his Lego army in solitude, naively assuming he's preparing for some kind of brick apocalypse, or I could use this pre-existing passion of Legos to entice him to a new topic of study. I choose door number two, thank you very much.

Here's where the strewing comes in. I start by laying out some headphones next to his play area. Next I set my smartphone on a kid-friendly podcast or audiobook app and casually mention he can have some time to listen to an episode all by himself while he plays with Legos if he wants to. He loves audio dramas and chooses a series about the life of Robert E. Lee. A few minutes into the story, he realizes this is the very same Lee I had mentioned when I came back from a whirlwind trip to Gettysburg, Pennsylvania, a few weeks earlier.

I had returned home laden with maps, photographs, souvenirs, and stories of a nation divided. We sat on the floor and retraced the turning point battle. He had listened intently then. But now after building and listening and building and listening on and off for the entire thirty-minute audio story, he's mesmerized. He rushes to our home library bookshelves and begins culling a stash of Civil-War-related titles. The next hour finds him lost in a literary retelling of Lee and Grant and their opposing armies. Somewhere in the mix, he lands on Lincoln. He learns of his presidency, his obsession with cats, and his insatiable appetite for chicken casserole—little-known facts found in a presidential trivia book. All these quirky and incidental details of Honest Abe lead to a lively discussion at the lunch table.

He spits presidential potpourri at us, rapid fire. "Did you know that the *S* of Harry S. Truman doesn't stand for anything? Truman never had a middle name. And William Taft was so overweight, 350 pounds to be exact, that he actually got stuck in the bathtub once. Can you believe that? Jelly beans were Ronald Reagan's favorite candy. In fact, the blueberry-flavored jelly bean was created in 1981 in honor of his presidential inauguration. Do we have any blue jelly beans, Mom?"

After lunch, he gathers craft supplies and a set of dice, spreads them out on the living room floor, and begins to make a homemade game of presidential trivia. He makes question cards, fake money, and an elaborate game board filled with colored squares. With his project in hand, he rallies his siblings to play a round or two. While playing, someone turns on another audio drama. And before you know it, my son's thoughts drift to Vikings and their European invasions.

The following is a list of simple ideas and activities you can casually suggest to your child in order to sneak learning into even the craziest of days.

Encourage your child to . . .

- Start a blog. Set the security to "lock" so that only invited friends and relatives can view it.
- Solve a hangman puzzle.
- Complete a MadLib story.
- Start a collection.
- Begin a line-a-day, five-year journal.

- Make a stop-motion video using a free stop-motion app.
- Create a pet habitat in a large glass jar.
- Write to a penpal or a deployed soldier.
- Take a nature walk.
- Hide or seek a geocache in your area.
- Open and keep track of a savings account with allowance or gift money.
- "Adopt" a missionary family by sending them letters, praying for them, and learning about the country and culture they are serving.
- Participate in the Great Backyard Bird Count. (http://gbbc.birdcount.org/)
- Write a novel during NaNoWriMo. (National Novel Writing Month)
- Recreate the construction of a famous building using blocks or other materials.
- Create a comic strip.
- Learn to make a variety of paper airplanes by consulting a step-by-step book or watching an online video.
- Make several small boats out of various materials, and test the float-ability of each.
- Create a floor plan for an indoor fort, and then build it.
- Plan a scavenger hunt for a younger sibling. Write or draw age-appropriate clues.
- Create a time capsule of your year, and bury it in the back-yard.
- Make a flip book.
- Try to replicate a famous painting.
- Plant a container garden.
- Learn a new handcraft by watching an online video.
- Volunteer to be Mom's sous-chef for the day.

- Build a puzzle.

- Shadow dad at work for a day.

- Attend a free presentation or workshop at a local library, community recreation center, or state park in your area.

- Visit the local farmer's market.

- Write out journal prompts on slips of paper, put them in a jar, and use them as inspiration to write short stories.

- Look at a coffee table book of Norman Rockwell's illustrations, and discuss the cultural and historical relevance of each picture.

- Create a word collage to describe your family using scraps from magazine headlines.

- Create a secret code, and encrypt messages to family and friends.

- Listen to an age-appropriate news podcast.

- Plan the week's grocery list.

- Answer the questions of a trivia game.

- Keep a calendar record of phases of the moon, weather patterns, or seed growth.

- Mark places of interest on an inexpensive map. These can include hometowns of friends and families, previously visited vacation destinations, and locations of key events in history.

- Take public transit as a family, navigating routes and travel time.

- Double the ingredients of a cookie recipe, and bake a large batch.

If cultivated, one passion can lead to the next that leads to the next. Like the mouse. The cookie. Every single time. Educating your kids shouldn't have to drain you or leave you feeling pulled from both ends. A child's curiosity can be his best teacher, allowing you to cheer from the sidelines. In this way, homeschooling can actually create calm in your current chaos.

However, should you feel dead to homeschooling because of the struggle that surrounds you, remember that God can resurrect anything. Pray He resurrects your love for your children, your calling, your commitment, and remember that this moment doesn't define your entire homeschool. You are more than your worst days. Nothing is ever too far gone for His redemptive power. He is always working even when it doesn't seem like it (John 5:17). He might seem complacent or sedentary, but He's not. Remember, Jesus was perfect and yet God's plans for Him still included a cross. "Not my will, but yours, be done," He said to the Father (Luke 22:42). Following God's will to teach your children at home doesn't mean everything will go exactly as you have planned. But it will always go exactly as *He* has planned.

The Struggle Is Necessary

Unfortunately, the Devil's play is often distraction. He wants to draw you away from God's good plans for your homeschool by making you feel defeated in the midst of them. He wants your fears and faults to take center stage. Remember Christ's words, and let them talk you off the ledge: "In this world you will have trouble. *But* take heart! I have overcome the world" (John 16:33 NIV, emphasis added). That *but* is the bridge that spans the gap between a test and a testimony. It's what turns a victim into a victory.

Just like you, your kids are going to have fears and faults too. And dare I say it, they're going to fail—in school, at work, in relationships. Failure is part of the deal of living. Don't deprive your struggling one of failure. That's how he'll grow. That's how he'll learn. No one ever learns nearly as much from the good stuff of life. We all learn most when we're allowed to try, fail, and get back up again.

Although it's hard to watch the struggle, especially when help is within reach, remember this: God didn't miss a stitch when He knit your child together. In praying that He keep all the hard things away from your struggling one or even expecting that He will answer such a request, you are denying your child the opportunity to be sanctified. In fact, according to 1 Thessalonians 4:3, you are robbing him of the very will of God. That's not to say that sanctification only ever comes through struggle, but that it *often* does. When your kids are allowed to struggle and see God working, they begin to stretch their own faith wings. Without the struggle, there would be no flight.

Remember the butterfly from my son's science project? He (or was it a she? Who can know?) took off with a perfect dismount from the branch. It took some time. It definitely took some struggle. But eventually, its wings did what they were designed to do. They flew. Had my son or I helped—had we removed any part of the difficult process—the butterfly would surely have died. The struggle was necessary. Christ's struggle was necessary. And perhaps your struggle is necessary too. But stay tuned—the good flight is coming!

PART 3

The Solution

Our society has made an idol of getting things done,
making that our top cultural priority.
But instead of asking, "Am I doing enough?"
why not ask, "Am I doing what's mine?"

————————————————

JAMIE MARTIN
of SteadyMom.com

9

It's Homeschool, Not School-at-Home

Most mothers who choose to homeschool do so because they want to provide something different for their children from what the other guys are offering. They assume that simply taking the road less traveled will make all the difference. Their kids will be happy, healthy, and well-educated. But somewhere along the way, they begin to notice the battle scars of a bad year, or maybe a string of bad years: the slumped shoulders, the downcast eyes, the sighs that exhale months of frustration. They wear them. Their kids wear them. Somedays it seems like even the dog wears them.

Can I be really honest with you? The kind of honest that might sting a little? *A different result* is kind of the collective heartbeat of all the mothers who have chosen to homeschool, yours and mine included. And yet so often we allow our past experiences and expectations of school to hitchhike into this new journey. "Real" school and "real" teachers are all we know. So we use *their* plans, *their* methods, *their* benchmarks—and single-handedly sabotage our own efforts. We foolishly use the map of the traditional way but expect to end up at a better destination.

It's time to get rid of the unnecessary baggage to your homeschool day—things that have just been weighing you down. This is freedom day. You don't have to be chained to the long-held but misguided beliefs about education that haunt you like the ghost of school past. Homeschooling was never intended to be school-at-home. The traditional model with all its formulas and figures is burdensome. So many of the practices are necessary and good *over there* but only because of the specific challenges of teaching a classroom full of children at the same time. Those same practices, when used *here* at home, constrict. Square peg. Round hole. Like an anchor threatening to pull you under, borrowing from "real" school can ruin your homeschool. If you're to survive, and better yet thrive, you'll need a new way of looking at teaching and learning at home.

The World Is Your Classroom

Setting up your entire home or even one room in it to look like a classroom will put you on the fast-track to feelings of failure. Sitting at a desk will not make your child an academic any more than standing in the kitchen will make him the next winning contestant of "Top Chef." The two are not tethered to one another. The same goes for other atypical school tools like chalkboards, learning centers, or the educational posters that grace the walls of most North American classrooms. While all of these can help to organize and motivate learning for the masses, they are more of a distraction and hindrance to learning at home.

A homeschool works best when it is family-friendly and welcoming to all members of the home. Caging older children in a designated "classroom" all day presents three obvious problems to homeschooling. First, if you have little ones who are not yet of school age, you will have to decide whether to (A) rope off the room with yellow caution tape and send the little ones into other areas of the home to fend for themselves or (B) invite them into the school space and run the risk of hurricane-hands yanking books off shelves and upturning science projects. The former poses serious safety concerns, and the latter creates unnecessary chaos and frustration.

Second, a home "classroom" can easily make you feel like an overworked piece of taffy. The jobs of playing wife, mother, and teacher get separated into zones, pulling you in a million different directions—from the schoolroom to the laundry room to the schoolroom to the kitchen to the schoolroom to the home office and back again. But by spreading school all around and allowing your children to learn wherever you happen to be, you can lead the homeschool day but not be chained to it. You can prepare lunch *while* listening to your first grader read aloud, or fold a load of laundry *while* reviewing the eleven body systems with your middle schooler.

Last, a "classroom" can inadvertently shape a lazy learner. If his learning always happens in a certain space, at a certain time, and with certain tools, your child will begin to think that learning can only ever happen that way. Kids who are allowed to sit at the dining room table, lounge on the couch, lie in a hammock in the yard, or even sprawl out on a blanket at the park will see that learning can happen anywhere, at any time, and in many different ways. Through homeschooling, the world can be a classroom. Your child can form a one-piece life because his living and learning get to be fused together.

Granted, it is helpful to designate specific spaces for storing all the books, papers, and learning tools that inevitably accumulate during the homeschooling years. But this may be done simply by placing a few bookshelves in a child's bedroom, converting the dining room china hutch into a school cabinet, or relinquishing a kitchen cupboard for art supply storage. Don't take the *home* out of homeschooling by forcing a classroom into it. That's a fool's errand that will only end in disaster.

The "S" Word

As the late author of more than sixty books and articles on human development Dr. Raymond Moore once asked, "What is the evidence that [traditionally schooled] children actually do get along better?"[1] Through extensive research and after analyzing over 8,000 early childhood studies, he found that the overstimulation and noise that happens when you jam a large number of kids together often makes children anxious. It creates a poor learning environment and can cultivate behavioral problems. As a champion of homeschooling, it was his opinion that kids are better socialized at home, by parents, not at school with other children.

Let's set Dr. Moore's research aside for a second and just unpack the facts. By its very definition, socialization is the ability to behave correctly in lots of different social settings and to interact with lots of different groups of people. Riddle me this: how often does the average second grader get to interact with anyone but his teacher and other second graders during the typical school day? Once at midday recess, if at all. Will "socializing" with thirty other six-year-olds teach *your* six-year-old how to converse with the elderly woman he'll encounter at the doctor's office? Nope. Will those same six-year-olds be able to help put your child at ease when he's asked to introduce himself to your new neighbor? Probably not.

A school is not an accurate cross-section of society. Forced association is not socialization. When else in life will someone only associate with other people born the same year he was? Never, once he reaches adulthood. Real-life relationships are diverse. They include lots of different kinds of people from all different ages and stages of life. Homeschooling, because it's not based on an institutional model, better mimics the real world.

Granted, educating a child at home does have the potential to be insular. There are those who have taken the privilege to an unhealthy extreme, folks who have drawn a clear line in the sand and who with the unyielding grimace of a dictator, double-dog-dare anyone to cross from one side to another. But that's certainly the exception, not the rule.

Without the time-consuming extras that inevitably come with managing a large group, homeschooling can give the day a long leash, allowing kids to participate in social activities of their choosing. From co-operative learning classes to organized field trips, nature groups and entrepreneurial clubs to sports teams and private lessons—these opportunities get kids out in the world, where they can meet and form connections with people of all ages, in all walks of life, and in many different occupations.

Some would argue that homeschooled kids are "weird" or socially awkward, and that's sometimes true. But one could say the same about many kids in the public school too. *Weird* is often more about nature than nurture. There are shy kids, bold kids, introverts, extroverts, confident ones and self-loathing ones, socially graced and socially awkward children in every schooling choice. Chances are, the shy homeschooled kid would still be shy in the public school because he's just shy. That's how he was made. The public school, with its sometimes unhealthy social hierarchy would probably just push the shy one further and further into his shell. Can we all agree that the world is full of "weird" adults, most of whom attended traditional schools?

Homeschooling can be a greenhouse that allows your child to grow into the very best version of himself. His wardrobe choices never have to be influenced by the "popular" kids. He may ask questions and discuss topics in an anxiety-free environment without fear of violence, bullying, or teasing. He can develop self-

> Homeschooling can be a greenhouse that allows your child to grow into the very best version of himself.

confidence and independence without ever having to learn under the weight of peer pressure. He'll never have to experience the stress of premature parent/child separation that some children experience at age five and can be encouraged to hold onto childlike innocence and silliness without being forced to mature faster than necessary. Other kids will not help your child grow to be a self-assured adult comfortable in his own social skin. Only adults can do that.

And since when did socializing become the goal of school, anyway? I thought school was for education. At least that was the goal when I was a kid. I can't tell you the number of times I got into trouble in the public school for "socializing" with my friends during class time. My teacher would wag a contemptuous finger and remind me to keep my mouth shut.

Offering opportunities for socialization is part of high school—with team sports, extracurricular clubs, dances, etc. But many of those opportunities can be opened to homeschooled teens without blending in any of the darker elements that sometimes surreptitiously slide onto campuses across the country, such as bullying, illicit drug use and underage drinking, weapons, suicide, sexting, and exposure to pornography. If homeschool kids don't "fit in" with that kind of society, well, that's kind of the point!

Homeschooling has provided my children with the gift of genuine socialization with others and, most importantly, with each other. In building a foundation of sibling togetherness, I'm nurturing friendships that will last for a lifetime. They love hard; they play hard; and they also fight hard. Feelings get hurt. Conflict ensues. Arguments erupt. Since my kids are not pulled away from each other for six to eight hours a day, they can't ignore the real struggles that happen in relationships. They must face them head on. Yes, they fight, but that also means they get to make up and experience biblical restoration. They can't just walk away or pick a new person to play with on the playground. They must learn to resolve problems and redeem relationships, life skills that are lacking in many adult friendships and marriages today. This time spent together is a training ground for *someday*.

Some Christians would counter with the "be in the world and not of it" argument as if just being in school equals evangelizing. Evangelism is not just a worthwhile goal; according to Mark 16:15, it is a command. As Christ-followers, we have the gift of salvation and know its value. We should obviously want to share such good news. But if we're looking to the classroom to be the simple solution for spreading the gospel, wouldn't sending our children to say a Muslim or Buddhist school be an even better ministry field than a free public school that might already have some Christian witness present? As I mentioned in chapter 2, however, not every five-year-old of Christian parents is even saved. And not every Christian tween and teen is spiritually mature enough to be thrown into the deep-end of culture in order to toss out lifelines to others. Homeschooling provides a great training opportunity for grounding children in truths that will prepare them to be salt and light in the world now and later.

I count it a privilege to be able to come alongside my kids as they encounter secular thinking and immoral lifestyles in the world around them. I can help shape these experiences and inform their ideas using Scripture. My homeschooled children are still very much "in the world," finding opportunities to discuss truth and philosophy, not just with one another or in our homeschool co-op, but in their neighborhood friendships, at summer camp, with their unsaved relatives at family gatherings, and even at parachurch events and organizations such as on mission trips or while serving with me at the local homeless shelter or soup kitchen. Like all Christian children, homeschooled or otherwise, my kids are growing up in the bright light of the gospel and are learning to apply it to the world around them. These formative years are their training years, providing opportunities for spreading the hope of Jesus to a hurting world while my parental help is still within reach.

Tests, Grades, and Other Unnecessaries

I remember loathing the weekly book reports assigned to me in my second-grade class. Each week, I'd pick up a new-to-me book and be transported to far off places where I'd meet fascinating people. I'd get lost in the language of literature only to be dragged back to reality when those dreaded book report pages were handed out. My teacher meant well. The forms were her simple way of assessing the comprehension and completion of the class.

To her credit, she added cute little clip art to the reports and awarded scratch-n-sniff stickers whenever appropriate. (Scratch-n-sniff stickers were like childhood gold on the 1980s playground. There was an entire underground market for them by the swing set every afternoon. Don't tell my mom.) But in the end, those mimeographed report forms were, to me, nothing but joy-killers that made an entire room of reading hopefuls disdain the very idea of reading. Reading became *work*, so no one wanted to do it anymore, myself included.

Sadly, so many homeschoolers repeat this dismal scenario in an admirable attempt at assessing reading comprehension. While I think there are definite benefits to teaching the skills of writing an expository book report in the upper grades, I don't see the point of assigning them to elementary kids. They're about as interesting as a houseplant and usually just end up crippling a child's love of reading.

Herein lies the plain, simple problem with book reports: they are designed for classroom use. They are an unfold-and-inflate method for one teacher to prove the reading frequency and understanding of twenty or thirty children. But as a homeschooling mother, you see your child read every day. You watch him as he physically turns each page. If you're curious about whether or not he's actually comprehending and internalizing what he's reading, you don't need to drill-and-kill with a worksheet, you just have to have a conversation.

Leading with "How did you like the book?" will probably only earn you the canned answer, "It was good." To develop deep and meaningful dialogue, you'll need open-ended questions instead, ones that can apply to any book from *Green Eggs and Ham* to *War and Peace*. That way, even if you haven't read the book yourself, you can still jumpstart a lively discussion about it. Here are a few of my favorites.

Ten Discussion Questions for any Book

1. What new idea or information did you learn from this book?
2. What was the most upsetting part of the book?
3. Were you satisfied with the way the book ended? Why or why not?
4. If you were to write the book, how would you change it?
5. With which character did you most identify?
6. How could that character change in order to develop the story better?
7. How does reading the story now, in this moment of history, change the story from the author's moment?
8. What emotion do you think the author wanted you to feel after you finished the book?
9. What led you to believe that?
10. What is the biggest point of tension in the book?

Book reports are just one of the million little "real" school methods that can exhaust your child's home education and leave you both feeling limp. Tests, grades, and grade levels are also on the list of usual suspects. We've all been conditioned to view them as a necessary part of education because they come from the large operating system of public schools that is so familiar. But they have very little, if anything, to do with real learning.

Grade levels help to corral children of similar age, size, and learning ability into a manageable herd. Our current classrooms evolved from the work-to-war system developed in Prussia (former Germany) during the eighteenth and nineteenth centuries and were popularized in the United States by education reformer Horace Mann. Then in the early twentieth century, school districts were restructured and small, one-room, rural classrooms were consolidated and replaced by larger urban schools. We were an industrialized nation that needed a labor force familiar with the factory model, so grade levels became the standard.

But grade levels don't have to be the standard for homeschoolers. Forward motion, constant learning, and the continuous building of the mind should be the goals.

> Forward motion, constant learning, and the continuous building of the mind should be the goals.

While the grade level I've slapped onto my daughter's state-required school district letter says *ten*, any number I assign to her is really just a loose suggestion—something to tell the talkative older lady who might happen to quiz her while standing in the produce aisle some Tuesday morning. According to the public school, because of her age, she's supposed to be in ninth grade. But she's actually doing college-level vocabulary and logic, eleventh-grade math, tenth-grade grammar and science, and ninth-grade spelling. It seems a bit complicated, but it's not.

Maddie, like all of my children, excels in certain areas and struggles in others. Homeschooling affords her the freedom to learn right where she's at. She doesn't have to be held back because thirty other kids need more review. On the flip side, she doesn't have to be dragged along to the next topic when she hasn't quite grasped the first one.

It would be impossible for one traditional classroom teacher to advance or withhold several dozen children without the assistance of obligatory plumb lines like grades. The same may be said of tests. With a test, a teacher can see at a glance what a child has learned versus what she has taught. She can get an accurate picture of how one child's knowledge stacks up against that of his peers and create a concrete, unbiased report of progress to show his parents.

Take the average spelling test, for example. The point of a spelling test is to show how many words a child has memorized in comparison to the number of words that were taught that week. Typically, the test is administered, then graded, recorded, and handed back to the child. A new set of words are taught the following week. But isn't the point of a spelling "class" to teach spelling? If a child misses five words on his test but is then immediately pushed onto the next week's word list, he'll never actually learn to spell those five words. What, then, is the point of spelling class? In a school with a class of twenty to thirty students, the teacher uses a test to assess progress only; that teacher can't shift to a dozen-plus spelling assignments in order to accommodate each student's readiness to move ahead.

Standardized test results show that homeschooled children are simply better educated than the national average. If those tests can be correlated with student learning, then why not choose an educational approach that delivers better results? The statistics also show something else of even greater importance: Homeschooled children are more likely to stay connected to their family and faith. The average Christian student who attends a public school will stop attending church during college and many will disown the Christian faith (see Souls in Transition *by Notre Dame sociologist Christian Smith). Why then, should Christian families not choose an educational path that strengthens faith and family bonds?* [2]

DR. CHRISTOPHER PERRIN
cofounder and CEO of Classical Academic Press

In my homeschool, on the other hand, I don't teach spelling *words* in order that my children can pass a test, or so that I can compare and contrast their skills with those of other kids. I teach spelling *skills* so that they can each become good spellers. I have the luxury of noticing which spelling errors keep cropping up, so we can work on those particular skills.

I realize that sometimes tests and assessments are state-mandated by the old guard. They are unavoidable. Here in my state of Minnesota, I'm required to administer annual achievement tests. This yearly ritual continues to prove to be pointless. But I'll play puppet if I must, knowing that a piece of paper can't possibly inventory true intelligence.

I give you Exhibit A. Several weeks ago while administering said compulsory test, I noticed that my second grader marked a very simple social studies question wrong. The question asked something like, "Which picture shows the correct way to eat soup?" The corresponding answers showed a picture of a child using his mouth to slurp the soup right out of the bowl, a child using a fork to eat the soup, and a child using a spoon to eat the soup. My son selected the picture showing the child with the fork. Not wanting to tamper with the results of the test but curious to know his reasoning, I asked him why he marked that particular answer.

"Because the soup in the bowl has lots of long noodles in it, Mom. And remember last week when you made that really noodle-y Japanese soup? Remember how you said I could eat it with a fork if I wanted to because I couldn't keep the noodles on my spoon? I just thought it would be easier for the boy in the picture to eat his soup if his mom lets him use a fork, too," he said.

My son chose the picture with the fork. Of course, he was right. But unfortunately, he was also wrong. If we're being honest, however, we'd have to admit that Japanese noodle soup would be easier to eat with a fork. The results of the test didn't actually measure his reasoning ability any more than it measured a whole host of other important skills like his creativity, self-control, loyalty, faithfulness, determination, and courage—skills he has worked hard to master all year long. It didn't because it couldn't. Tests weren't made to measure such things.

Knowing All Things

It's easy to believe that when your kids get an *A* on those tests you get one too, as if your value is directly related to their abilities or inabilities. Be very wary of that ledge, Mama, lest you fall into a pit of your own making. Should your state require you to record grades, or should you feel compelled to keep them in order to ease your fears, please hold them loosely. Don't allow your child's success or lack thereof to determine whether you get a *pass* or *fail* as a teacher. Their outcome is not necessarily your outcome in this thing. You can plan until your eyes cross, overspend on curriculum and supplies like you were making a down payment on a Prius, rock every single lesson, and watch as some parts of their learning still completely flatline.

By fastening your success to theirs, you are giving yourself far too much credit and far too much blame. In assuming you are the key ingredient in the recipe for success, you are implying that you have to be an expert at absolutely everything in order to impart all of that *everything* to your child lest he end up with an irreparable gap in his education.

> By fastening your success to your children's, you are giving yourself far too much credit and far too much blame.

But you don't need to teach all the stuff. It's actually impossible for anyone to teach all there is to learn in the world, and that includes all the "professional" teachers in the school system.

Those of us who came through the traditional school model are proof that educational gaps are unavoidable.

Like every compliant eleventh grader in Phoenix, Arizona, I took a consumer mathematics course, and yet I never actually learned how to fill out a check until I was standing in line at Walmart trying to buy toilet paper for my college dorm room. I aced human anatomy in junior high. Pinky swear. And yet I was nearly thirty-seven, clinging to my daughter's hospital bedside in a pediatric cardiac ICU before I truly learned the functions of all four chambers of a human heart. Most shocking of all is that while I was introduced to the seven-times family in third grade and was expected to memorize them, I never truly learned any of them until I taught them to an entire class of third graders decades later.

According to my teachers, I was an *A* student in school— top of my class. I earned an academic scholarship to college and was later asked to speak at the graduation ceremony. Ironically, I walked out of the auditorium that warm May day holding a piece of paper certifying that I knew enough to teach young minds all they needed to know. And yet I knew very little.

There were many gaps in my public school education. Seventy-five-years-worth of studies have shown that students in the traditional school model retain only a small fraction of what they learn from year to year.[3] I was no exception. And chances are, neither were you.

But gaps get filled in time. Information is learned when it's needed. When I needed to know how to fill out an IRS 1040, I asked an accountant friend for a crash course in tax filing. When I needed to take an accurate resting pulse, I watched a YouTube video. When I needed to drill the seven-multiplication table, I learned right along with my students. Necessity truly is the mother of invention. Whenever I've needed to know something, I've always found a way to learn it.

The same will be said of your kids someday. Should you forget to teach them some "important" something, rest assured they will learn it when they need to. Should you flounder in your curriculum choices for a couple of years and find yourself hopping from one program to the next, you'll probably create a few loose ends in learning, but those loose ends will all get tied eventually. Twentieth-century British educator Charlotte Mason once said, "Self-education is the only possible education; the rest is mere veneer laid on the surface of a child's nature."[4]

To that end, your goal is really not to be a teacher, but a coach. Every major-league baseball coach stands outside the foul lines mentoring, cheering, and inspiring the athletes they are hired to train. They are not necessarily better athletes than the players. If that were the case, they would be playing instead of coaching. Their skill is influence and inspiration. Their job is to point their students, or in this case athletes, further down the path of success. The goal of a coach should always be to see the athlete surpass him. The same should be said of a teacher. Don't allow curriculum detours or your own academic shortcomings to plant seeds of fear or failure.

> Your goal is really not to be a teacher, but a coach.

Homeschooling bravely doesn't mean you have to teach everything. It just means you get to decide what, where, and by whom something is taught. Over the years, I have outsourced a number of subjects. I've enlisted the help of friends and neighbors who have had a much stronger passion or aptitude for one particular area of study than I did or do.

Whenever living, breathing mentors were unavailable, I purchased digital and video-based courses instead. Mandarin Chinese, piano, baseball, robotics, geometry, physics, personal finance, magazine editing, and typing—these were not things I was qualified to teach. So I didn't.

I don't feel the least bit guilty about having deferred the

weight to someone or something else. Farming out some subjects or topics is not the white flag of surrender. It's just an admission that I am homeschooling with *my* kids and *my* life in mind.

And that's the very clarity that you need, my friend. That's the necessary paradigm shift that has to happen before you can homeschool with bravery. This is your home. This is your school. If you've been operating from any other premise, you've been spoiling your own efforts. No wonder you've felt fearful. No wonder you've contemplated a forfeit.

As homeschooling pioneer John Holt so famously wrote, "What is most important and valuable about the home as a base for children's growth into the world is not that it is a better school than the schools, but that it isn't a school at all."[5] There are many more entry points to education than the one the public school has taken. You don't have to follow anyone else's agenda. Let go of whatever commandments you have painstakingly chiseled on a tablet of your own making. Remember, it's homeschool, not school-at-home.

10

A Guilt-Free Year

Twenty-first-century mothering is hard work. Granted, you and I are parenting with privilege. The digital age has provided time savers and cheat sheets like no other generation before us. But information overload is not the yellow brick road we'd all hoped it would be and has actually bred a generation of second-guessers and chronically unsure parents. We're given mixed and often competing messages at every turn.

Don't helicopter parent. Give your kid room for goodness' sake. But never let him walk to the neighbor's house alone. There are predators lurking around every corner. Safety first. This isn't 1983, after all.

Be sure to sign your kindergartner up for this summer's softball, gymnastics, Lego robotics, ballet, and soccer programs. The grand total will be in the same ballpark as her first year of college, but if you don't get her started early, you'll ruin her chances of ever going pro. Remember though, free-range childhoods are best. Tamp it back a bit. Geesh, you can't control her every moment. How will she ever learn independence?

Maintain a tight grocery budget, utilizing coupons so you can walk out of the store with them owing you money. You want to be a good steward, don't you? But remember to buy only organic and locally grown items because that $9 apple might be the only thing *separating you from cancer. Good gracious, don't you care about your health at all?*

Co-sleep, breastfeed, and wear your baby. Except don't. Your baby needs to learn to self-soothe. Calm down, Mama. You're spoiling him. And also, no red dye 40. That's Satan's son.

What's Yours to Do

For the love of all that's mentally healthy, make it stop, please. All this social hysteria is enough to make me see double. These are complicated times for moms, to be sure. Couple all that cultural mom-shaming with homeschooling, and it's no wonder that bravery seems just out of reach for most of us. I, for one, don't need extra emotional clutter and guilt. I've spent far too much time in those tedious spaces.

Confession time: I was boots on the ground, deep in the guilt trenches with my first child before I ever realized how uncomfortable those shoes really were. I trudged mile after mile, limping to keep up at times. Then I had four more kids, and I quickly realized that perfect mothering was not sustainable. And also, cereal could be served for dinner when necessary. (You're welcome.) I learned to be gentle with myself—kind even.

Jeremiah 31:3 says that God draws us all with unfailing kindness. Society might use guilt, shame, and social media slactivists

> *She who feels smart enough, organized enough, equipped enough to homeschool is delusional and puffed up. This job demands love, patience, and kindness that are not of this world, but are fruits of the Holy Spirit.*[1]
> LINDA LACOUR HOBAR
> author of *The Mystery of History*

in an attempt to modify motherhood. But God uses kindness. These days, kindness seems out of place. Old fashioned. Forgotten. But kindness is always God's play because that is His nature. Kindness moves my heart and helps me chase the peace I so desperately crave.

In His kindness to me, God's shown me that in trying to do everything perfectly, I end up doing a lot of things with mediocrity. In His kindness, He's revealed the idol I've molded out of my mothering. In His kindness, He's encouraged me to stop wondering if I'm doing enough and has given me the courage to ask, "Am I doing what's mine to do?"[2]

> In His kindness to me, God's shown me that in trying to do everything perfectly, I end up doing a lot of things with mediocrity.

God continues to use kindness to draw me in my motherhood—to show me when I've cloaked all those social pressures in pretty superlatives to make them sound more believable. Again and again, His kindness has helped me see how and when I've made parenting and teaching harder than it needs to be.

Linger over Learning

Not too long ago I received a message from a new-to-homeschooling mother who, whether she knew it or not, was desperate for a little kindness too. She wrote asking for suggestions for preschool. She needed direction. Her message went a little something like this: "Jamie, I'm heading to a local homeschool convention. I've got money in my pocket and preschool on my mind. What should I buy? What are your top preschool curriculum choices?"

I imagined her crouched over her computer screen, pen

and paper in hand, ready to jot down all my sage suggestions. I taught preschool in a traditional classroom for three years and had homeschooled all five of my own kids through the early years, she knew. Certainly, I'd be able to point her to a perfectly curated boxed set of this or that. Right?

After letting her question percolate for a moment, I tapped out my reply, "Open-ended toys and a library card, that's all you need. Linger together, and learning will happen."

"But what about language arts? What should I be using for math? Which workbooks would you recommend?" she questioned.

We went back and forth for a few moments, she with her questions and me with my simple answer. It was clear that my easy formula for preschool success was not what she was looking for. I could almost see her raised eyebrows through my inbox. She had no time for my platitudes and well wishes. She needed answers, and she needed them yesterday!

I couldn't blame her. I remember running on that same treadmill years ago when my daughter approached those delightful pre-years. I thought that if I did something, lots of formal somethings, I would give her an education that would count. I would be able to call it school. So I plunked down piles of money and bought some of those cut-and-paste type workbooks that are so "essential" for preschoolers today. I filled bins and buckets with educational activities, seat work, and whatever else my trusted scope-and-sequence recommended. I wanted to get it right. This was her education, after all.

In my defense, my contrived curriculum plan was a result of my pedagogy—the many years I had spent earning my education degree and being trained by experts. Traditional education had hammered its "tradition" into my head and hardwired me to make everything about learning more difficult than it needed to be.

Preschool as Americans know it today with students being cajoled into finishing their "work" before they may play and school boards tossing around words like "school readiness" and "early literacy" is a relatively new addition to the educational landscape of this country. Up until the 1960s with the launch of the federal Head Start program, there was no *pre* to school. Children were allowed to be children and encouraged to linger in the way children naturally learn, through play. Preschoolers of yesteryear were never "schooled."

The truth is, nearly fifty years of research regarding early school entry still doesn't show solid evidence that formal preschool is even necessary. In fact, some studies show that by third grade when the majority of students have transitioned from the learning-to-read phase to the reading-to-learn phase of their education, the playing field completely levels. Kids who never had any formal preschool perform just as well on normative tests as those who attended Head Start or other preschool programs.[3]

Ironically, while there's very little academic benefit of preschool, there are plenty of downfalls. In most cases, the statistics of burn-out, boredom, and restlessness are staggering.[4] Children who enter formal learning in the formative preschool years have a much higher chance of losing their enthusiasm and love of learning than those who have been allowed to maintain the freedom of play.

Mr. Fred Rogers once said, "Play is often talked about as if it were a relief from serious learning. But for children play is serious learning. Play is really the work of childhood."[5] Five trips around the preschool block have taught me that kids are born with a natural curiosity. The moment you or I try to push a rigorous agenda, we push them away from real learning. Good books and lots of lingering—this is the cream that will always settle to the top of education.

Unfortunately, even when we feel a conviction to keep things simple for preschoolers, we often change our minds when those same kids move on to kindergarten, or first grade, or twelfth. The moment that *pre* is dropped from school, we feel an urgency to make learning a more complicated prescription. *Rigor* and *rigidity* become the primary markers of our homeschools. Fanciful plans and notions of what *could be* lure us into cramming every subject, topic, and idea that we want our kids to learn into one school year. We coerce and bully our kids into completing the daily checklist and position their education to look like a threat: *You're gonna learn this or else!* Learning quickly becomes a dogfight with moms and kids squaring off in opposite corners, each vying for more control. When that happens, no one wants to homeschool anymore—not moms, not kids.

Admittedly, the toys and the books may have to change and evolve as our kids get older, but the concept of lingering over learning through play and personal interest shouldn't have to. You don't need to squeeze a lesson out of everything or force-feed anyone. In fact, you can't. But you can set a feast of ideas before your kids and let them taste and see. They won't be interested in everything, mind you, and some things may not stick. But instead of casting their nets a mile wide but only an inch deep, they'll be encouraged to linger—to reach deeply into the interests and gifts God has already hard-wired inside of them.

> Set a feast of ideas before your kids, and let them taste and see.

There's where you come in. Your job is to provide space and time for a child to exhaust a topic; it's never just to push him onto the next. You are to help cultivate a growth mindset by lingering, repeatedly exposing him to similar ideas and materials until he can claim mastery. Greek philosopher Aristotle once said, "Excellence is an art won by training and habituation. . . . We are what we repeatedly do. Excellence, then, is not an act but a habit."[6] Lingering allows a recessive skill to eventually become an active one.

In lingering over a few things, your child may miss out on

others. But that's to be expected. Mastery of skills requires focused attention. Innovators and world changers throughout the ages have contributed to the great conversation of humanity not because they have known a few things about everything, but because they've known everything about a few things.

I see that in my kids every day, especially my son. At eight, he has created a portfolio of award-winning pencil sketches and has the ribbons to prove it. He's not a child prodigy. He wasn't born with exceptional art skills. He's just an ordinary boy with extraordinary commitment to keep lingering until he can claim mastery.

Last year, when my husband and I saw him take an interest in sketching, we purchased a light pad for him for Christmas. My husband is a professional artist and knows from experience that the only real way to learn how to draw is to practice tracing real works again, and again, and again until you can create them yourself—lingering over learning.

For months, my son traced pictures of giant squid. Nothing else. Just squid. We had read about them in science that year and he took a shine to them. He traced squid in bed. He traced squid in the car. He traced squid while sitting on the couch. Eventually, he could practically draw a lifelike squid in his sleep.

Instead of sampling and surveying many things, he chose one. Slowly over time, with much lingering, the squid-mastery gave him the confidence to try drawing other animals. Fish, at first. Then birds, and horses, and even spiders. He became an expert of nature art and can now pretty much draw any animal under creation.

And so it goes with learning. Lingering changes things. Focused attention on passions and true gifts changes things. Homeschool should never be a spectator sport with you doing all the work and your kids watching idly from the sidelines. They have to lean hard into lingering themselves. But you can provide them with the tools, time, and encouragement they need to learn well. You can stop insisting on rigor, and let them explore, play, and create while still using toys and books.

In other words, it's perfectly acceptable to let your son read *Farmer Boy* for the fifth time in a row, or your daughter watch not one, but all eighty-three ukulele videos on YouTube, or your whole family camp in that volcano unit in science for the entire school year, because that level of lingering will steer their learning to confidence. Inch-by-inch, stitch-by-stitch, they will not only learn how to learn but also how to love it.

> Stop insisting on rigor, and let the children explore, play, and create.

Go Right to Go Left

One of the perks of homeschooling is that it provides flexibility to minister to others. That's the case with my family, anyway. Our near-elasticized schedule has allowed me and my children to volunteer during typical school hours when others are just not available to help. In this way, my kids have been able to learn academics, life skills, and a ministry mindset right alongside me in a natural way. If you've been homeschooling for any length of time, I'm sure you can say the same.

Learning at home has probably given you and yours extra life in your days with which to share with others. But there's a flip side to that coin. I think you and I can both admit that we try hard, harder, hardest to be all things to all people. Our days can be full, but they're not always fulfilling.

The busy mandate of our current culture has created a ratings mindset in all of us. We now calculate our worth by how many items we can check off our to-do list. Homeschooling brings our productivity to a whole other level, practically demanding that we squeeze fifty-six-hours-worth of work into a twenty-four-hour period. Busyness is our drug of choice because public praise is often the side effect. But there's a difference between doing something out of love and doing something to feel loved.

Your identity cannot be found in your ability to meet someone else's quota. You don't have to set yourself on fire just to keep others warm. God constrained Himself when He took upon human flesh. He gave Himself physical limitations. If God recognized the need to do less for a time, then why shouldn't you? Why shouldn't I?

I have a sneaking suspicion that Jesus walked through life a little more slowly than you and I do. Could it be that He knew how to say *no*? He was never distracted by the tyranny of the urgent but gave His time to the most important things. He knew busyness does not necessarily equal productivity.

> Busyness does not necessarily equal productivity.

Like Christ, in order to give a full *yes* each day, you have to learn to be okay with saying *no* to things, sometimes even good things. Think of this as a "go right to go left" kind of situation. Instead of constantly making a to-do list, I'd encourage you to make a *don't-do* list. Decide right now what you don't want to do with your time and actually write it down—in ink.

There are obviously going to be many unavoidable tasks that tug on your day, especially if you have other large commitments besides homeschooling that demand your time like a job outside the home, ministry responsibilities, or caring for aging parents. But by prayerfully making a don't-do list at the start of each school year, you are mentally preparing yourself to be able to give a hard and fast *no* to those things that deplete you and leave you with little to give to homeschooling. You'll have more room for the yeses that matter most.

When asked to join this committee or host that event, you won't even have to expel mental energy weighing pros and cons.

You'll simply point to your don't-do list to find the answer. What's more, you won't have to carry one ounce of guilt or regret, because you'll know that all the items on the list were already given careful consideration. That's not to say you can't ever veer from your list and say *yes* to something you had originally deemed a *no*. Your Plan A should only ever be written in ink, not in stone.

You'll have to wage a one-woman war on your schedule because no one else is going to do it for you. Fun fact: most people think homeschooling moms are just sitting around watching Netflix in their jammies all day. When they want something done, they ask a homeschooling mother, because what else could she possibly have pressing on her time? And while most well-meaning friends won't ever fully understand just how time-consuming the ministry of homeschooling actually is, you do. You know.

> Wage a one-woman war on your schedule because no one else is going to do it for you.

The next time you're asked to volunteer or take charge, don't be afraid to give a polite, "No, thank you." Use it as a complete sentence, and dole it out with bravery. Trust me, the wheels aren't going to come off that "important" thing.

Good Enough Is Good Enough

As a homeschooling mom, your life probably looks radically different from the lives of other women. Your home probably does too. I know mine does. At times, those differences can be discouraging.

It often feels like I'll be playing one giant game of sardines until the end of time. Unlike most of my friends, I am with my children for a great majority of the day. There's no escaping them. They are always there. I get no sick days, or holiday pay, or time off for good behavior. It's just them and me. All the live long day. And while I sincerely wouldn't have it any other way, I sometimes wish I could hire a substitute teacher. My house feels understaffed most of the time.

On paper, I know what a privilege it is to walk alongside my children each day. I get to be present, *really* present, and to pour into them deeply. But in practice, I struggle with the weight of it sometimes.

Adding insult to injury, many days my home looks like it should require a hazmat suit for entrance. I'm half expecting a producer from "Dirty Jobs" to show up on my doorstep requesting permission to film a scene or two for an upcoming episode. Clearly, something apocalyptic must have occurred within these walls to create such mess, right? I've come to realize that a less-than-tidy home is the occupational hazard of homeschooling. And I'm okay with that.

This past year, my husband and I have replaced two couches, a lamp, an entire room's worth of carpet, several rooms' worth of paint, and two bunk beds with all the trimmings, while beginning major demolition on a back patio. My needs-to-be-repaired-or-replaced list is lengthier than the tax code, and it seems that "clutter and dust" have inadvertently become my new decorating theme. (I've got my fingers crossed, hoping that *messy* will be the new *clean* in all the spring design catalogs. But that's probably a gross overreach of optimism.)

If my children were sent off to school each day, I'd get a respite. I'd get the solitude my soul craves some days. My house would sit empty. My furniture would have a longer lifespan. My rooms would stay clean. But then what? Although it would be nice to be able to actually use my antique buffet table to serve food instead of as a science project display case, Proverbs 14:4 helps adjust my perspective: "Where there are no oxen, the manger is clean, but abundant crops come by the strength of the ox." One day my "manger" will be clean, but it will undoubtedly also be empty. So should you happen to drop over unannounced, please excuse the mess. I'm preparing for abundant crops someday.

Don't mistake my sincerity in this. I'm not advocating for laziness. I'm not dismissing duty. Like most mothers, I want to create a home that feels like a haven—a safe place for others to land. I, too, operate more efficiently at the intersection of Clean and Organized. I'm merely encouraging you to embrace scruffy hospitality and to recognize that homeschooling can and should shift your priorities a bit. You simply can't wrestle a huge time commitment like education into an already jam-packed schedule. That's not a cop-out. That's not an excuse for disorganization. That's just the simple laws of physics. To add a new thing into a crowded space, you first have to take something out of the space.

In order to do homeschooling well, you'll have to set other things on the back burner or at least be willing to accept Good Enough. Deciding that something is good enough isn't an excuse for slacking off or lowering standards.

Good Enough just acknowledges that what you used to find very important isn't necessarily as important in this moment. Good Enough accepts the needs of your home without judging or feeling judged by the needs of someone else. It's the grace you need to prioritize what's important to you without feeling guilty. There's no need to wear yourself out chasing peace. The only way to outrun the regret of chaos is to finally accept Good Enough.

Self-Care Is Group Care

When you are tired, out of fuel, or just overwhelmed with homeschooling, don't quit. Just learn to rest. Homeschooling doesn't have to make you invisible. You still get to be you. You still get to have separate passions apart from your home and your school. In fact, it's best if you do. Self-care is absolutely essential if you hope to make homeschooling sustainable.

No matter how busy you think you are right now, there's always room in your day for you. *Busy* is actually just a myth anyway. A person will always find time to do the things that matter most. So start admitting that you matter. Start penciling yourself into your plans and make your hobby a non-negotiable on the schedule. That doesn't necessarily mean you have to block out an entire day to recharge. Even a few minutes here and there can go a long way to water a thirsty soul.

> Self-care is absolutely essential if you hope to make homeschooling sustainable.

If you don't currently have a hobby, start shopping around for one. What did you like to do in your free time before having kids? Before homeschooling? What activity makes your body lift in breath or droop in exhale when you even think about it?

For me, the answer is reading. I've been a Word Nerd all my life and find that reading a good book fills in my empty, depleted spaces like very few things. Last year, I managed to carve out enough time to read thirty books. These did not include the dozens upon dozens of books that I read aloud to my kids for fun, for history, for science, for Bible, and all the rest. These were books just for me. And lest you think I've got some kind of monopoly on the clock, let me set you straight. I'm a work-at-home, homeschooling mom. I'm currently buried somewhere under a book deadline and have what feels like 0 seconds of "extra" time. But today, like every day before it, I was given twenty-four hours. It's my choice how I spend every single moment.

Reading is a non-negotiable. It's self-care that ends up benefiting everyone in my house. When I read, I'm not only able to teach from a place of abundance because I'm well-read on a vast number of topics, but I'm also able to stay sane. I'm fairly certain I'd end up acting like a Mad Hatter if I didn't have at least ten minutes to read each and every day.

Because reading is a must, it is a permanent line item on my schedule. In the same way I ration out time to teach math, language arts, history, and science, I relentlessly carve out time every day to read. It's my way of gently peeling off the pressures of the day.

Each day, no matter how busy, contains fringe moments—little bits of time that will leave you sitting, waiting, loitering. It's easy to squander that time sending texts, checking Facebook, scrolling Instagram. But you don't have to be a digital prisoner. The choice for how you use your fringe moments is yours. A cell phone is an easy distraction because it is handy. It's always with you.

In the moments when you could reach for your phone, what if you reached for your hobby instead? Admittedly, fringe moments don't always come with a warning. They are random and unpredictable. That will mean that you'll have to have your hobby always-at-the-ready and possibly get a little creative in order to claim that time efficiently.

While not always fashion-forward, I make sure I carry a purse large enough to fit at least one book inside (or three). When I'm standing in line at the DMV or waiting around at basketball practice, I can read a few pages. Five minutes here, five minutes there doesn't seem like a lot, but in spending even five minutes reading every single day, I claim many hours each year turning pages in the fringe moments. And that's more than enough time to read a few books.

Having a desire to do something that fills you is not selfish. Even Jesus snuck away to be refueled. "And he said to them, 'Come away by yourselves to a desolate place and rest a while.' For many were coming and going, and they had no leisure even to eat" (Mark 6:31). Does that sound at all like your life right now? Do you barely have enough time for leisure or even to eat? Your hobby doesn't have to bleed your homeschool. You can enjoy something simply for the sake of enjoying it. That's not shallow or trivial. Self-care adds to homeschooling even if it looks like it only adds to you.

You have to know your role. You cannot carry what's not yours to carry. Stop wearing someone else's expectations and judgments. That outfit never looks good on anyone. Walk in the freedom that is yours through the kindness of Christ. Linger over learning, say "no" when necessary, be content with Good Enough, and let this be your guilt-free year.

Your Spot on the Wall

Last year at an afternoon fundraising event in a neighboring town while sitting at a table with a handful of moms—some of whom homeschooled and a few who did not—I found myself in a clash of words. One of the non-homeschooling mothers whose children were all grown and launched leaned in toward the rest of us and, like a trial lawyer making her case, declared to the group why she thought homeschooling was defective and would eventually lead to ruin.

Apparently, her husband was a counselor and currently had two homeschool grads as clients. According to her "sources," these two desperate souls had mental health issues and were seeking professional guidance because they were struggling to *adult*. They weren't assimilating into the "real world," she assumed, and pointed to homeschooling as the cause. Like she had a black belt in fear-mongering, this woman went on to say that those of us who had chosen to homeschool were only moms, not teachers—unskilled or ill-equipped for the magnitude of the job of educating.

Fine. I'll scratch that itch, I thought. I began to dig deep, preparing to deliver some verbal annihilation. Before she finished her misguided diatribe, I was already locked and loaded with rebuttals, standing ready to take my victory lap. It didn't matter that some random stranger had just stopped me in the supermarket the day before to commend me on how well-behaved and courteous my kids were or that the public librarian pulled me aside earlier that week to comment on how articulate my son had been when she was speaking with him. One snarky comment from this woman sitting across from me suddenly outweighed all the positive feedback I'd ever received about my decision to homeschool.

"I'll forget the very obvious violation of doctor-patient confidentiality for a second and not wonder why you, the counselor's wife, knows anything about these two individuals. Instead, I'll only ask you this: Does your husband have just the two clients then, or does he have more? And if so, is it safe to assume that all of his other clients attend or attended a traditional school? I would never say that a public school education would make a person want to see a counselor, but according to the logic of your own story, you would," I replied. This was just the start of the vitriol that began oozing out of my mouth the hot second she was done talking. I'll admit it was not my finest hour. I'm pretty sure everyone else in the room was second-hand embarrassed for the other moms at my table who had to bear witness to my unraveling.

I wish I could take it back. All of it. If I could hop in Doc Brown's Delorean and go back in time to that day, I'd do things so much differently. I'd just smile and ask if she could please pass the coffee creamer. That's it. I wouldn't unload. I wouldn't do any truth-telling. Instead, I'd let my silence speak powerful volumes. I didn't need to rally anyone to my side or change her careless opinion. Most of all, I didn't need to let my personal offense steal time and energy away from the kingdom work I was doing through my homeschool. I didn't need to do it, and neither do you.

Your Spot on the Wall

Just Keep Building

If you're a bit indecisive and shaky like me, the critics can easily spark your buyer's remorse. They shout from the curb while you're deep in the trenches doing the work. The Enemy will use their fault-finding words to distract you from your calling.

Let's not forget that Satan is focused. He wants to destroy God's work in your homeschool or at least make you limp while doing it. Outrage is often his weapon of choice. Stand guard against a victim mindset, though. Offense is a sneaky seductress. In time, she'll introduce you to her seedy companions: bitterness, unforgiveness, jealousy, and revenge—all of which will slowly chip away at what you've spent years building.

In Nehemiah 4, we see how the distraction of critics can threaten the work. Under the authority of King Artaxerxes of Babylon, Nehemiah returned to Jerusalem to rebuild the outer wall of the city that had been destroyed by King Nebuchadnezzar 150 years earlier. With provisions ready, he rallied the Israelites to reconstruct the nearly two-and-a-half-mile-long wall around the city.

The builders labored for fifty-two days before finishing the work. But in that time, they came upon much opposition. The adversaries of the Lord repeatedly tried to thwart Nehemiah's plans. They used gossip, harsh criticism, and even the threat of bodily harm to spread fear and failure across the job site. They wanted to distract the builders, blur their vision by pointing out potential risks. "For they all wanted to frighten us, thinking, 'Their hands will drop from the work, and it will not be done,'" Nehemiah concluded, "But now, O God, strengthen my hands" (Neh. 6:9).

Nehemiah would not let the naysayers derail him from his God-given task. He encouraged the people to find their spot on the wall and just keep building. When the opposition came on strong and the people began to fear again, he raised their spirits with six of the most powerful words ever spoken: "Our God will fight for us" (Neh. 4:20).

151

If God is for you and your homeschool, dear one, who can be against you (Rom. 8:31)? School choice is one of the most polarizing issues in the mommy wars today. It's a hot topic, to be sure. But it doesn't have to be so toasty. When two roads diverge in a wood, there will always be well-meaning folks pushing you toward one way or pulling you toward the other. But education is not a popularity contest. It doesn't really matter which way is the choice of the majority. The question is, which road will lead to God's ultimate plans for you and your kids?

Criticism will come. They are an unavoidable part of life. Even Jesus experienced the sting of rejection during the ministry He was called to undertake. He was laughed at, scorned, second-guessed, and criticized. But, the reactions of the people didn't negate His heavenly call.

> God is your defender; you never have to explain your schooling choices to someone else.

Homeschooling may have earned you the disapproval of others. But you don't have to show up to every argument you're invited to. Are you willing to surrender your reputation to God? Will you let Him have the last word? If God is your defender, you never have to explain yourself or your schooling choices to someone else.

It's Not *Us versus Them*

Dial back your defenses, and sturdy up a bit. If you're always coming in hot, ready to justify your decisions, you'll quickly burn up and burn out. Take my word for it. I've been in school choice conversations where the heat was palpable, where no one was actually listening, where the participants (myself included) were all mentally preparing rebuttals. Reloading. Taking corners, taking sides, and strapping on verbal gloves to prove points and jockey for right-ness. No one came out unscathed or converted.

Trust me, as a former teacher, I get an expected amount of raised eyebrows because I had the audacity to veer from the party line. People who feel deserted will naturally take offense and will broadcast that offense in very visceral ways. I can remember one particular stand-off that had me believing that the win would inevitably go to the one who could shout the loudest.

I was in a conversation with a woman at my church and mentioned that I homeschooled. Her follow-up question came with a bit of an accusing tone, "What is your background?" She was a teacher and wanted proof of my qualification to educate. It felt like someone was attacking my tribe. My neck hair bristled, and I instantly began looking for wagons to circle.

"I have a teaching degree," I stated rather flatly. She had poked the bear. I felt as if she was not only attacking me but also every other mother who had ever chosen a different path for her child's education. I mentally prepared a fiery monologue to prove that WE'VE GOT THIS!

But as I opened my mouth to unleash a tirade, I remembered this one simple truth: Education is not an *Us v. Them* situation. When I could unstrap my fighting gloves for a moment, I could see her raw vulnerability. Just as I was acting like a cornered squirrel because I felt threatened, she was too. She was a lovely woman who had dedicated her career to teaching children with excellence in the best way she knew how and felt hurt that I would prefer a different way—as if by rejecting her choice, I was rejecting her. In her hurt, she had built a wall of protection. Her defense was to find some loophole in homeschooling that would make the struggles of the public school classroom look smaller by comparison.

After all, fear is not tethered just to homeschooling. Those other moms who send their kids to a traditional school nurse their own fears, faults, and failures. Don't forget that anger is often a secondary emotion to fear. It is a defense mechanism, a way for them to deflect attention from their own emotional wounds. Engaging in a verbal tussle will rarely convict hearts or change minds, it will usually just irritate and inflame pre-existing pain. For the sake of living out the gospel, can we put our anger to rest? Second Timothy 2:23 reminds us, "Have nothing to do with foolish, ignorant controversies; you know that they breed quarrels."

The problem with using other people's opinions as a barom-eter for life is that everyone has a different one, homeschool educators included. If we're being honest, we'd have to admit that sometimes we homeschoolers can be just as condemning of those other moms. We thump the Bible harder as if God endors-es our choice more than theirs, assuming He must surely be on our side and that the public school will sacrifice their kids to a

It is a brave endeavor to try to give to our children what we were likely not given ourselves—a good education. It takes courage to resist the raised eyebrows, skepticism, and criticism of others to do something you know will be difficult and for which you sense you are not well prepared. That's bravery that some may call folly. And yet it seems more clearly to be folly to enroll our children in failing schools that will likely pull our students towards vice rather than virtue. It requires no small amount of courage for those of us who were not educated well to pull our children from schools where there stands a small army of professional teachers ready to teach our children—for free. It takes courage to resolve to learn along with our children, slowly recovering the education for which we secretly long ourselves.[1]
DR. CHRISTOPHER PERRIN
cofounder and CEO of Classical Academic Press

life void of Christ. We too have something to crusade for, or so we think.

We go in with guns blazing, touting homeschooling as the answer to everyone else's problems. We see a friend's public-schooled child falter socially, spiritually, or academically and pridefully announce that homeschooling is the answer—the quick fix that will right every wrong. We see our "perfect" curriculum and our "perfect" methods and our "perfect" well-ordered plan and begin to prescribe it to our friends and their obviously-in-need-of-change children. We place homeschooling on the throne of God and forget that change comes only through Him. He changes hearts. And truth be told, He can do that with or without homeschooling.

If you find yourself speaking in bullet points, firing shots, and making friends run for cover, ask yourself, *Is my eternal goal to lobby for change or to love a neighbor?* Be careful lest you win the battle but lose the war. R. W. Ward in his commentary on 1 and 2 Timothy and Titus has this to say to those who choose to flaunt their religious liberties and parade them around like doctrine: "In the end, disputing about words seeks not the victory of the truth but the victory of the speaker."[2]

> Yours is not to worry about someone else's call.

God doesn't need another blow horn; He needs a doer. He needs hands and feet willing to do the work He has called them to. Yours is not to worry about someone else's call. As Christ said to a preoccupied Peter in John 21, if your friend or neighbor chooses to send her kids to public school, "What is that to you?" Lay down your weapons and just keep building your spot on the wall.

The Voices That Matter Most

"You're not a teacher," the critics will say. "So how can you teach?" If you haven't heard that drum banging yet, be ready. You will. When they're casting their stones, that's usually the first one the naysayers lob out.

Perhaps it's true. Perhaps you're not a teacher according to state standards. No matter. Who cares what a piece of paper says or doesn't say? We've been friends long enough now that I think I can just shoot you straight with no apologies. Here goes: If you're being pushed around by fear, you're not listening to the Voice that really matters.

If God has called you to homeschool, He has called you a teacher. Full stop. As you look in the mirror and see all your shortcomings, know that God sees something entirely different. God sees you for who you are becoming, not for who you are right now.

That's God's way. He forecasts victory because He can see all the way to the very end. He called Abraham the "father of many nations" before he and his wife Sarah ever conceived one child. He called Gideon a "mighty warrior" before the man ever set foot on a battlefield. He dubbed David as king when the kid was nothing more than a shepherd. And Peter? Well even in the midst of Peter's cowardly denial, Christ nicknamed him the "Rock," and made him a leader of the fellowship of Christ-followers.

Over and over again, when the world only saw misfits—a motley crew of cast-offs—God saw so much more. He used the mediocre every time He performed the miraculous. He raised up flawed people to do the work of building, not because they were ready *right now*, but because He knew that with His transforming power they would be ready *someday*.

You might not call yourself a teacher. The state might not call you a teacher. Your in-laws might not call you a teacher. But God does. He speaks into your life like only the Word Made Flesh can do. As the miracle-maker, He sees past the right-now you, looks ahead to the end of the story, and sees the completed you. He sees you as a teacher even when you don't. That's part of the miracle He wants to create in your homeschool.

God forecasts victory because He can see all the way to the very end.

You have nothing to prove if your identity is fully rooted in Christ. I realize that you can't always unsubscribe to the negative voices. Sometimes the loudest criticisms come from parents, in-laws, and lifelong friends—all necessary and unavoidable relationships. Those wounds cut deep, to be sure. But might I suggest that you dismiss those specific opinions with grace and begin to listen for the voices that will help you build?

Safety can come when you place yourself in fellowship with those who have a common vision. Nehemiah did not work all by himself. He did his part, no doubt. But he also strategically placed people around him who were willing to pick up a hammer too.

If your current circle is zipped up so tight that you are getting cramped in a camp of your own creation, then start expanding your circle. Begin looking for other homeschooling moms to link arms with. Join a moms support group, a co-op, or even an online community that will stand to your right and to your left, building the wall right alongside you. (There's a lovely tribe of moms at The Unlikely Homeschool that would welcome the chance to spread their arms out to you.)

You need to start seeing the success of homeschooling in others. You need to see other people doing the work too. If you don't see it, you won't believe it, and the Enemy will try to pry you from your post. Community is necessary in homeschooling, for you and for all the other moms around you. If you feel attacked, they probably do too. They need your support just as much as you need theirs.

Not sure how and where to find community? Well, let me

give you a map to follow. The next time you feel the sting of criticism, send a note of praise to another homeschool mom. Start banging *that* drum, and you'll eventually hear an echo. No one has ever said, "I feel too encouraged today." Iron sharpens iron. Deep calls to deep. To have friends, you must show yourself friendly as Proverbs 18:24 says (KJV). Send encouragement out in big, lavish waves, and the ripple effect will be far reaching. Make a phone call, send a text, write an email or a social media shout out.

You'll rarely just stumble into a vibrant community. More often than not, you'll have to build one from the ground up. Such was the case when I started homeschooling all those years ago. I looked around for sisters and found a dozen or so women who appeared to be living in the same relational bankruptcy I was. We were all clearly in need of someone, anyone, willing to co-sign on our decision to homeschool. One of us just needed to make the first move. I was naive enough to volunteer. I sent out a few invites, baked a pie, and waited anxiously one night for one or two ladies to show up. Twenty women, most of whom I had never met, came. They squeezed into my teeny-tiny living room like circus performers crowding into a clown car and spent the evening filling up on coffee and community.

My part in the whole thing was aggressively mediocre. I didn't decorate or plan a lengthy agenda. I poured drinks and pointed folks to the bathroom. But somewhere in the middle of all the mingling, I mustered up enough bravery to reach out to one or two women, which in turn gave them the bravery to do the same. Before I knew it, I had formed a monthly homeschool moms support group filled with allies, which is still going strong today, ten years later.

G. K. Chesterton once said, "A dead thing can go with the stream, but only a living thing can go against it."[3] If you show up when someone in your homeschool sisterhood is least expecting it, you'll awaken a tribe that will help you swim against the raging current of criticism. Get in line behind the gospel, extending love, grace, and a listening ear to those who need it, and you will never lack for community, homeschooling or otherwise.

You get to pick which people to listen to, friend. You get to decide which voices to ignore. Stop being pushed around by fear. Pick your tribe, and be drawn by love.

> Get in line behind the gospel, extending love, grace, and a listening ear to those who need it, and you will never lack for community.

Just Keep Your Head Down

You can drape yourselves in the tattered cloak of the perceived judgment of others and trudge around in it all the livelong day, wrestling for shreds of approval from everyone else. Or you can homeschool like you know you are already pre-approved by the One who called you to do it. The choice is yours.

Like in the story of Mary Magdalene, you will probably suffer criticism for "wasting" your life or the lives of your children on Christ. People will say that your talents, time, and energy would be better served in other ways than just homeschooling. But pouring out your best for what He has called you to do is never a waste.

Your God will fight for you. This was the rallying cry of the wall-building prophet all those years ago. Let it be yours too. Stop striving. Stop proving. Your heart will forever be restless in this world until you can learn to rest in Christ.[4] You do *you.* Don't worry about the *you* they want you to be. Let God strengthen your hands for the work. Keep your head down. Keep your eyes on the wall, and just keep building.

12

The End in Mind

This past February marked the twenty-third annual Winter Olympics. Since we live in the near-tundra where temperatures are only above freezing for about two minutes a year, the winter games have a way of stirring up a special kind of crazy in my family. We host large viewing parties to celebrate the opening ceremonies. We watch and rewatch every single event like it's our part-time job. Some of us have even been known to spray-paint the Olympic rings onto our snow-covered rooftop to prove our loyalty to the rest of the world. These are just the facts. I've come to terms with them. Let's move on.

Needless to say, I had such high hopes for the Winter Olympics. I envisioned a sixteen-day long unit study complete with a few crafts I'd found on Pinterest, biographies of famous athletes, a geographical study of the hosting nation, and maybe even a backyard slalom or two. But when the day of the opening ceremonies finally arrived, I came down with a horrible flu bug. The Olympics were shelved and eventually forgotten.

A week later when life returned to normal, I had a choice: I could beat myself up for missing out on half of the games, or I could extend myself grace and just pick up the homeschool baton where I had left it. I set the dream of craft projects aside and hunkered down on the couch with my kids to watch the remaining events. If I were to make a Venn diagram showing what I had hoped for regarding homeschool during the 2018 Winter Olympics versus what actually happened, there would be very little overlap. But, in the grand scheme of life, who cares? The gravity of the games and our time spent together as a family were still marked in our hearts and minds. Imperfect plans that actually get done are always better than perfect plans that never happen.

Unfortunately, though, high hopes are often the final wave that submerges a drowning homeschooling mom. She dreams of what homeschooling *could* be like, *should* be like, *must* be like—and when those dreams don't materialize, she writes *failure* across the whole thing, including herself.

I know a number of homeschooling moms who have decided homeschooling isn't for them. They've packed up shop and have enrolled their kids in the public school. Now I'll not assume that I know every detail of their decisions, but after talking with many of them, I can say that their stories share a common theme: the whispers of disappointment, of unmet expectations, of failure. These moms were not completely satisfied and want their money back.

I can't say I blame them. I too started this journey hoping to find some sort of silver bullet—a quick fix, twelve-step-style program for great learning—as if education can ever be bought at the drive-through window. At my first hurdle, I shook my head like a wounded animal, looked around, and wondered, *What kind of rabbit hole have I fallen into?* But the real problem wasn't the hurdle, my friend. The real problem came long before that when I just threw a bunch of plans at a page and expected them to stick. I started the journey by pulling on loose threads with no real thought to what I wanted to make with them.

Define Success, and Plan from There

Nothing will ensure longevity more than determining what your goal is. Just as a runner starts a race by knowing exactly where the finish line is and in what direction he has to go in order to get there, you need to know what you're aiming for and point yourself in that direction.

What is your metric for success? If you're anything like I was all those years ago, you probably plunge into each new school year blindly, not really knowing which way you're even running. It's easy to do. Right now, you're in the crowded years. You're a slave to the daily demands of a small circus of your own making—dirty diapers, toddler meltdowns, soccer practice, and dentist appointments. But you won't always be. As the poet Sir Henry John Newbolt wrote, "We build for the days we shall not see."[1]

To start out well, you'll need to plan with the end in mind. You'll need to look past these busy years to the years when your kids will be launched adults. Finish this statement: "I will feel like I have done my job as a homeschooling mom if my children grow up to . . ." What do you hope those future people will be like? Start from the end, and back up to right now. What can you be doing today to point their feet to the right end?

> To start well, plan with the end in mind.

Ask yourself, "What's my *why*?" Why are you homeschooling? Why did you find this type of education worthwhile or better than sending your kids to the professionals down the street? Why did you want to keep your children home and invest so many years and so much money into this thing? Determining your *why* will help you to see what is most important to you. It will give you laser focus on the things that will build into your family's homeschool. Your *why* will help you establish clear boundaries, clarify long-term goals, simplify your spaces, spend money wisely, and build contentment because it will act as a litmus test for every decision. It will become a simple mission statement—a tool to help you plan your homeschool around the home that you actually have, not the one you wish you had.

For instance, if you are homeschooling in order to have daily influence on the spiritual growth and maturity of your children, then Scripture and character training should play a large part in your homeschool day. If providing a more realistic social experience is a goal, then you'll probably want to register for a local co-op or schedule regular visits to an area nursing home. If cultivating a really enriched learning environment is your priority, then you'll want to plan for hands-on, messy projects and sign your kids up for extracurricular activities like music lessons and art camps. Obviously, certain subjects are non-negotiable as determined by your state. But maybe they can be a smaller cog in the wheel.

After you have clearly defined your *why*, begin to align your homeschooling decisions with it. If something doesn't fit, no matter how perfect it seems to be for every other family, remove it from your mind, your schedule, your shelves. Everything you do—every resource you choose, every time commitment you make, every extra you squeeze into the day—should reinforce or run parallel to your answer for "Why am I homeschooling?"

You only have one life to live with your kids, so live it with purpose. Don't squander the days with poor decisions. Everything in this world will cost you something, including homeschooling. Sometimes the cost is larger than you'll ever even realize. Sometimes the cost is the number of moments you've spent and will never get back. Your *why* can help you determine whether each decision you've made for your family is worth the high cost you'll have to pay for it. It will help you to see your stewardship, or lack thereof, more clearly.

Your *why* will help you create an uncomplicated homeschool. You'll be able to see at a glance what your homeschool *is* and what it is not supposed to be. Once you determine your *why*, be willing to honor it. Make a list of everything you're currently doing and then set that list up against your end goal—your *why*. Scratch out anything that doesn't line up. Edit everything but the essentials.

Full disclosure here: I'm still a work in progress in this area. If truth be told, I'm an addict in need of a support group. *Hi, my name is Jamie, and I sometimes lose sight of the end.* I tend to grab at lots of great things in hopes of packing them all into my almost-perfect school day. I'm sure I don't need to tell you what happens as a result, but since as an addict I need to name and claim my vices, I'll give you the abridged version: I become a frazzled, ill-tempered woman, carrying a weight that will eventually pull me under the waves.

It's about People, Not a Product

Every time I scroll my newsfeed, I read of another victory for homeschoolers: top honors in the national geography bowl, a perfect score on the SATs, a full-ride scholarship to an Ivy League school. The headlines are replete with wins in our favor. But is this how we should define success?

When I cast a clear vision for my homeschool and return to my *why*, I can quickly see the error of that line of thinking. Don't get me wrong. I don't believe there's anything shifty or unsavory about academic achievement. But as a Christian, I think I'd do well to have a different endgame, to look to the finish line of Christ. Scripture says that as Jesus grew, He increased in four specific areas: wisdom, stature, and favor with both God and people. He did not come fully formed; neither do our kids. Homeschooling should be more than just a tool to serve minds. If academic success is the final goal, then a public

Training kids is soul-work.

school is the easiest, straightest path. But training kids is soul-work. In our efforts to steer minds, we can't forget to mold hearts.

Homeschooling is about producing people, not a product. I don't know about you, but at the end of the journey, I want to look back and see lives well lived. Moments savored. Souls shaped. Kids who have increased, not just in wisdom and in stature, but also in favor with God and others.

It's so easy to get pre-occupied with spinning all the wheels and completing all the assignments. But I never want to sacrifice relationships on the altar of homeschooling. The world doesn't need another smart person. It has more than its share of those. What it desperately craves are people who can show kindness, compassion, honesty, and integrity. I don't just want God's plans for my homeschool to inform my kids, I want His plans to *transform* them. My children need Jesus more than they need a perfect education.

> My children need Jesus more than they need a perfect education.

Charlotte Mason once said, "Every day, every hour, the parents are either passively or actively forming those habits in their children upon which, more than upon anything else, future character and conduct depend."[2] I have to be willing to set the books aside sometimes and do the knee-bending work of eternity. I need to have the ultimate end in mind. That's not to say I'll do everything right. I won't because I don't. My children get to see my daily ugliness day in and day out. There's no escaping the truth of my depravity as a wife, as a mother, as a teacher. The awful truth of me is left open and exposed for them more times than I care to admit. But *that* truth is a gift. If I could somehow hide all my imperfections from my children for even a day, I would show them a woman who has no need for a Savior. I'd be a momma pointing them in the wrong direction.

A brave homeschool is not a perfect homeschool; it's a gospel-centered one. Granted, not every moment of home-schooling will feel like deep, mean-ingful soul-growth. But it will be. The unseen or unplanned lessons of character-building can be what sets a home education apart from all the others if you allow them to count.

> A brave homeschool is not a perfect homeschool; it's a gospel-centered one.

Most of the time, the lessons your kids will learn from the pages of their books are not nearly as important as the ones they'll learn from life. The other day while reading aloud to my youngest son, I came upon an old poem entitled, "Hearts, Like Doors, Will Ope with Ease." To the average person, it's just a silly little verse with an unknown author. But to me at that moment, it represented the entire point of why I chose to homeschool in the first place.

When I was five, I was assigned the role of Goldilocks in the kindergarten end-of-the-year pageant at my school. I'd like to say it was because of my Oscar-winning audition. But the more accurate truth is that I was the only blonde in the class. A brunette playing the title role would never do. Even at five and six-years-old, the whole class knew this.

About a month before the show, I lied to my teacher about something and as a punishment was stripped of the part. I was tasked to memorize and recite "Hearts, Like Doors, Will Ope with Ease" instead. My sin resulted in a consequence. I may not have been able to see the link between the two back then, no one had ever pointed it out. But at thirty-eight years old, holding a copy of that long-forgotten poem in my hand while reading out loud to my son, the truth was undeniable. The irony of seeing my five-year-old son staring at the sin of my five-year-old self was not lost on me.

If a classroom teacher had read that poem to my boy, it

would have been just another assignment, read and passed over for the one on the next page. But homeschooling gave it more purpose. It gave it eternal weight. Homeschooling gave me the chance to tell my son a simplified version of my kindergarten disappointment. We talked about lying. We talked about sin. We talked about how sin is a robber that steals so many things, including the small joy of playing Goldilocks. With the end goal in mind, I used that poem to point my son toward favor with God and humankind.

Why are you homeschooling? Is your goal to execute the perfect Winter Olympics unit study? Is it to ensure your kids have an impressive high school transcript? Is it to raise up the next Harvard graduate? While all of these are worthwhile dreams, I think they fall short of the true worth and value of homeschooling, which is to raise up kids who love God and love others—kids who can press hard into their faith. Remember, God is more interested in who your children are than what they grow up to become.

I wish I could give you a simple formula for homeschooling with the end in mind. But, you can't always tack a pretty system onto spiritual transformation. My best advice is to examine your daily liturgy. Ask yourself which homeschool habits and tasks are helping to shape your children in light of eternity and which are not. The pieces that will be the most significant and soul-shaping won't be flashy and entertaining. It's in the mundane, repetitive faithfulness—the liturgy—that character is formed.

> Character is formed in mundane, repetitive faithfulness.

The warp and woof of your homeschool will change each and every year. Your kids will be older, they'll have new interests, they'll have new struggles. But the liturgy—those foundational habits you've set into place to answer your *why* questions—should stay the same. These should be fixed anchors and have a permanent place in your days. They should be lived out in the lifestyle you have created and be done on purpose.

For instance, if you're hoping to raise children who are missional-minded, then what are you doing right now, this very day, to draw their hearts to share the gospel in your neighborhood? If you're wanting to grow adults with useful, blue-collar skills that can contribute both financially and physically to their homes, what experts are you introducing them to today who can teach them these practical skills? If you're aiming to develop effective communicators who will ask hard questions and articulate clear answers, then what conversations are you currently having with them that will develop that aptitude? Look ahead to the finish line, and find the best path to get there. Don't just rely on a worksheet or a textbook to do the job. Allow life to count. Allow the daily liturgy to count.

You are like the farmer carefully planting seeds that won't actually bear fruit until much later. The field might look fallow and dormant, but many things are happening just below the surface. Your task is to plant while the soil is rich and fertile and then have patience like the farmer, allowing the invisible, silent work to happen slowly over time.

Happily Ever After in God's Terms

Here is where you pour out all your hope and wait faithfully, expectantly, for it to grow. Homeschooling, like farming, doesn't always pay out immediately. But as Elisabeth Elliot once said, "Don't dig up in doubt what you planted in faith."[3] Don't fret or spend another moment wringing your hands. Every little bit of effort, every tiny ounce of consistency, every tiptoe step of forward motion will eventually add up to great things. That's not to say that everything will line up in neat little columns by graduation day.

But you can't just trust God with the plan, you also have to trust Him with the pace. Homeschooling might be only the beginning of their transformation. It's easy to think of homeschooling as a recipe. *If I can just whip and stir these ingredients together, follow these seven simple steps, and then set the timer for twelve years, I'll produce faithful, engaged Christians.* But your kids are not muffins, and you can't microwave sanctification. You have to be willing to accept the fact that homeschooling doesn't automatically ensure *fully formed* adults.

Homeschooling isn't the easy way. But you're not in it for *easy.* You have the end in mind and won't quit until the final push. At the end of the journey, you'll bear the stretch marks of homeschooling, the proof of your sacrifices and labor pains. And there will be pains. Homeschooling will never be without struggles, just as the public school will never be without strengths. You just have to decide that *these* are the struggles and strengths

I say that any mom who has a desire to educate her children and a willingness to put in the work (Yes, I said it!) to make that happen will absolutely be successful in homeschooling her children. It may not be easy. All days won't be apple pies, refrigerator-worthy art, cuddles and reading, and fun field trips, but if she is faithful to the work in front of her things will turn out as they should. Homeschool moms need community, professional development, and self-education. They have to model learning if they want to see it realized in their homes. When you have a mom willing to do that, no matter her current level of education, then the successful homeschooling will follow. [4]
PAM BARNHILL
author of *Better Together* and host of the *Your Morning Basket Podcast*

God wants for you and your kids and then press into them. Along the way, you'll make plenty of missteps, especially at the start. But you're allowed to not know what you're doing. You have permission to make wrong turns.

When you find yourself going the wrong way, double down and refix your eyes on the end. You're going to have to hold your goal out each and every day and then take small, intentional steps toward it like an elderly cat. Each day won't seem like much. Some days you'll see the needle move, and some days you won't. But consistency is key. Persistence and pluck will support and sustain you when no amount of know-how, talent, and gifting seems to help. All the while, you'll be wondering, *Did it stick? Did it work?* But the outcome is not up to you, my friend, only the obedience.

If you're obeying in faith, all your steps and your kids' steps will be ordered by the Lord, not just the pretty ones, not just the ones that go in the easy direction. You don't need to rest on your high hopes of homeschooling. You need to rest in your Most High God. If your children miss a step somewhere along the way, rest assured, He can and will redeem it. He is the Great Redeemer, after all. He can sift through each moment of your family's homeschool journey and repurpose any and all of it when necessary. He will not allow one moment to be wasted.

Case in point, when my husband ended his years of homeschooling, he did so with bitterness and brooding. He didn't enjoy his high school years and flung his distaste for it at anyone standing too close. As I mentioned before, homeschooling in the 80s and 90s was an uncharted approach to education.

> You don't need to rest on your high hopes of homeschooling. You need to rest in your Most High God.

Consequently, there were not many homeschoolers in his area to give him any sense of belonging. He spent many useless years of his life struggling with imposter syndrome, trying to prove himself to the world.

Let me be clear, my husband's parents did everything right while raising him. They were faithful to their calling. Let's not forget that even the most perfect parent had wayward children. God gave Adam and Eve every opportunity to obey, and they chose their own way instead. My in-laws wrapped their home with the gospel. In their love for their son, they believed, hoped, and endured. They didn't shrink or cower at his sins. They didn't look away. They moved toward him. They showed up time and time again when he needed them most. In fact, my husband would even now credit his dad's nightly family devotions as some of the most formative moments of his faith. His rebellion was not their fault. It was completely his.

Self-doubt sent my husband on some windy and slippery roads, all of which landed him in a pit with pigs. But though he tried, he could never outrun God. God was with him in the dark places and continued to use lessons he learned as a child during homeschooling to draw him back to the light of the gospel and the forgiveness that only comes through Christ. None of his instruction was wasted. None of the investment returned void. God used every moment of those years at home to create a foundation that held up even under unthinkable pressures. He was a prodigal son who came home with scars, but he came home.

The road for my husband wasn't straight. But God has taken that winding past and has given it purpose. What was once a burden to bear is now a talent he's using for God. Sin did not silence his story. Like the man set free from demons in Luke 8, he has returned home and is telling "how much Jesus has done for [him]." He's now convinced more than ever of the value of home education. He's a living testament of how God uses it for His glory. And that, friend, is the true endgame. Every part of your life and the lives of your children is to bring glory to Christ—to make much of Him—including homeschooling.

God continues to redeem the years the locust had stolen from my husband. He hasn't arrived in his faith, mind you. He's still a work in progress. But so am I. So are you. So are your kids. I don't share this to scare you, but only to remind you that homeschooling is only part of the journey. It's not the end. You cannot put all of your hopes in a formula or a particular educational choice. Remember, you're dealing with fallen people. Humanity is never tidy, even when it's grown in the greenhouse of a Christian home or a perfect garden. If you're willing, God wants to travel some long roads with your kids. Every mile will mean something, even the wandering ways and the missteps. It will all matter.

You can trust God with your child's future, even if that means that there might be winding parts along the journey. He will carry your kids from womb to tomb, and that includes all the parts that come after their education. Their stories belong to God and are covered by the blood of Christ. Homeschooling is not their savior, Christ is. So no matter what trials or temptations come their way someday, if they've put their faith in Him, the final line of their story will surely read, "Happily ever after."

13

Check the Box with Bravery

Will you fail at homeschooling? Will your perfectly selected, expert-approved curriculum fall short? Will all the letters behind your name—the decorated endorsement of this college or that university—turn out to be nothing but alphabet soup when it comes to educating your children? Yes, if you are going through the motions in your own strength. All of these are wood, hay, and stubble without the one variable that makes all the difference in the equation: God. You can scramble up on any platform the world cranes its neck at, but without God, all of those accolades, perfect lesson plans, or expensive curriculums will fall flat. No fancy trim work will be able to cover up a shoddy foundation. Just ask the prophet Elijah.

You'll find Elijah in 1 Kings 18. Look for the guy surrounded by skeptics. Fear and doubt were mounting in the hearts and minds of the Israelites. They had struggled for three years without rain. Drought had come as an unwelcome visitor and had unpacked for a lengthy stay. The parched and brittle land was a sad reflection of the souls of the people. They had sinned. But, as always, God had a plan to redeem and restore. It would take faith, however—the kind of faith that ignores the experts, dismisses the perfect formulas, and embraces the impossible. It would take the faith of one man standing alone against the opinions of the masses and trusting God to come through.

After watching the nation limp in spiritual complacency for far too long, Elijah challenged the false prophets to a showdown. Crowds of curious cynics gathered on Mount Carmel to watch as 450 prophets of Baal faced off with one lone man of God.

"Let two bulls be given to us, and let them choose one bull for themselves and cut it in pieces and lay it on the wood, but put no fire to it. And I will prepare the other bull and lay it on the wood and put no fire to it. And you call upon the name of your god, and I will call upon the name of the LORD, and the God who answers by fire, he is God" (1 Kings 18:23–24). With one taunting dare, Elijah invited the false prophets to prove the might of their god. And the prophets agreed to the terms. From morning until night they wailed, pleading with Baal to rain down fire. Their cries were met with silence, however. No fire came. Their expertise didn't produce what was expected.

Then it was Elijah's turn. He began to rebuild the altar of the Lord. It had sat for years, untouched, forgotten. It was now one jumbled heap of rubble. As he piled one stone on top of the other, the crowd pressed in. And here is where the story takes a dramatic twist. Scripture tells us Elijah dug a large trench around the base of the altar. After arranging a bit of kindling and the now-butchered bull, he instructed the onlookers to fill four pitchers with water. I can only imagine the awkward silence that settled on the mob as this madman of God doused the stones not once, but three times. The trench was flooded. The sacrifice was saturated.

The odds were stacked against him. Not only was he the clear underdog on the mountain that day, completely outnumbered by the prophetical experts, but he also single-handedly sabotaged his own sacrificial efforts by utterly defying the simple laws of science. Water and fire don't play nicely. Even if Elijah could summon his God and convince Him to send a roaring flame, no amount of fire would ever consume a waterlogged pile of wood. At that moment, Mt. Carmel was complete amateur hour. Elijah's was a rookie move. The people knew this. The false prophets knew this. I'm sure even Elijah knew this.

But Elijah didn't forfeit or fall back. When faced with the impossible, he prayed and simply obeyed. He called upon God to be big—bigger than the experts, bigger than the crowd of skeptical onlookers, bigger than his inabilities. He called for a miracle. And no sooner did the pleading words leave Elijah's lips than God rained down a fire that not only made bark out of that bit of brisket but completely consumed it. Nothing was left—not the bull, not the wood, not even the stacked stones. God's inferno erased any sign of that altar, lapping up the water and all of the doubts of the people. They fell on their faces in repentance, acknowledging that nothing is impossible with God (1 Kings 18:20–39). And immediately a rain cloud appeared on the horizon; the drought was over.

When the Odds Are Stacked against You

Mama who doesn't think she's smart enough, organized enough, equipped enough, fill-in-the-blank enough to teach her child, homeschooling just might be your Mt. Carmel moment. Here might be where your inabilities become glaringly obvious to everyone else. Here might be where the odds are anything but in your favor. Like Elijah's, yours may seem like a hopeless case.

You might march straight to homeschooling without a teaching degree. You may even come without a high school diploma. But even if you come with your arms completely empty because your entire schooling experience was dreadfully deficient, you can still homeschool your child better than the experts and naysayers that surround you. As they wag their fingers in contempt, present your small offerings with singular boldness, pleading with your God to be big. And without fail, He will be.

When your homeschool plan looks like a big jumbled mess, when you're drenched in doubt and called to deep waters, when all you see is the impossible, *that* is the very time when God will do His most impressive work. He's got a pretty good track record with lost causes and less-than circumstances. You might even say they're His specialty.

Present your
small offerings with
singular boldness,
pleading with your God
to be big.
And without fail,
He will be.

God is not sitting in heaven having a pity party over what He has to work with. You're not a disappointment to Him. In the same way He didn't have to use Elijah's work to bring the rain, He doesn't have to use you in your child's education. But He chooses to. He was a miracle-maker back then, and He wants to be a miracle-maker today, in your life and in the life of your kids.

When your abilities seem small, when you're surrounded by people who could do it better, when your time and finances and patience are depleted, bring your small offerings to Christ. Trust that He can take your simple loaves and fish and create a feast for you and your children. Your impossibilities will become twelve baskets full and overflowing in His hands.

If homeschooling is a part of God's good plans for you and yours, then you can trust He will not only make a way for you to do it successfully but that He already has. He's neither surprised nor shocked to find you standing on this particular Mt. Carmel, crying out to Him for a hot rain of help. He's been expecting it. If you're careful to look around, you'll see the stones and wood already laid out just waiting for you to build in faith and obedience.

> *You are perfectly designed to homeschool your children. God has provided you with everything necessary to do so. It may take a little effort to build a few skills here or there, but all good fruits require at least a little work. And, lucky you, there are more resources available to help build those skills than ever before! Even if you come upon a really hard challenge that you don't feel like you can overcome, there are plenty of people and other resources to help you remove that particular burden. You can do it!*[1]
>
> CINDY WEST
>
> founder of Our Journey Westward and author of *Homeschooling Gifted Kids: A Practical Guide to Educate and Motivate Advanced Learners*

Obedience Always Precedes the Miracle

God does not require your success, my friend, only your surrender. You're charged with simple obedience. God is in charge of the results. But you can't have one without the other. Don't believe me? Take a quick flip through Scripture, and you'll find that obedience always precedes the miracle. The fisherman's nets had to be cast on the other side before the fish would jump into them (John 21:6). The paralyzed man had to take up his bed before he could walk (John 5:8). The Israelite priests had to step out into the raging waters before it would part (Josh. 3:14-17). Obedience came first every time.

The best part about simply obeying in faith and trusting God's good plans for your homeschool is that obedience and trust take the pressure off of you. You don't have to be a math genius if you're not. You don't have to be impressively patient if you're not. You don't have to have lots of letters behind your name if you don't. You just have to believe God can and will provide—that He will take whatever small offerings you hold out and multiply them. You don't have to stand at the back of the line fearing the fish and bread will run out when you get to the front. They won't. He's got enough for you. He's got enough for me. Trust Him and just obey. The obedience always has to come first, then the miracle.

> Obedience and trust take the pressure off you.

God's in the business of turning all of our nothings into somethings. He's good at it. After all, He's had a lot of practice; He's been doing it since the very beginning. You know your homeschooling journey won't be easy. But God never promises an easy road even in the middle of His miracle. In fact, more often than not, the struggle is what He uses to draw us closer to Him and to show His might in the miraculous. The struggle is the trench full of water that makes the situation absolutely impossible without God. But the fact of the matter is, if you never needed to be rescued, you'd never fully know the Rescuer.

Feed Your Faith, Not Your Fear

Fear will never lead you well because it speaks in falsehoods and cannot be trusted. Doubt is a bully that will always try to knock you down. But here's the thing: if you feed your faith, your fears will starve to death.[2] If you fix your eyes on the Author and Finisher, you won't ever lack for bravery because He always completes the work He begins (Heb. 12:2; Phil. 1:6). Nothing is ever half done in His care. You might stumble forward, but He'll catch you and set you right again. Trust that if God has called you to it, He will help you do it.

You may not be the homeschooling mother others think you should be, but you are the homeschooling mother your children need you to be. God thinks so. He chose you for the job, after all. That's not to say you won't ever doubt again or that your days will all wrap up perfectly. You'll still misfire occasionally. It's only natural.

Some days will still leave you emotionally tone-deaf. Your kids won't always give their best, but then again, neither will you. Some weeks will feel like educational utopia, and others will make you want to spray Agent Orange on the whole thing and start again. But don't allow one bad day or even a streak of bad days to define your homeschool.

I'm going to be brutally honest. Even after all these years, I still fear. I still fear my kids will turn from their faith—that they will lose sight of eternity. I still fear I'll miss something and my failures will hold them back. That's the funny thing about fear: it's not usually connected to what is happening in this moment. It's usually a response to what may or may not happen in the future.

Bravery, on the other hand, exists in the present tense. It happens right here, right now. It's not a lack of fear, mind you. It's just a decision to do the thing even in the midst of fear. Bravery is the courage it takes to say with boldness, "Here is my homeschool, God. Here, too, are my fears, faults, and failures. They're Yours now to face, fix, and forgive." In my bravery, I might never say farewell to all my fears, but I'll face them.

All those years ago in the doctor's office when I checked the "other" box indicating my decision to homeschool, I was confronted by criticism. The "expert" thought that sending my daughter to the public school would be for her good. She stood tall in her white lab coat. She had the right tools, the professional proofs, and the crowd clearly in her corner as she attempted to make me surrender. Admittedly, it almost worked. I nearly doubted myself right into defeat. But instead of caving to my faults and failures, I realigned my focus and began feeding my faith, not my fears. I clung to the promises of Philippians 1:6 and became confident that He who began a good work would carry it to completion.

If I could go back and do that doctor's appointment all over again, I wouldn't bat an eyelash at that doctor's misguided remarks. I'd not only check the "other" box, I'd highlight it and underline it in red. Now I know God can and will weave all my imperfections together in order to perfectly shape my homeschool. I've seen the proof.

But what about you? How will you homeschool bravely? When faced with the firing squad—when you're desperate and drenched in doubt—how will you check the box in faith and not fear? Well, like Elijah, I hope you just show up. Against impossible odds, do the work and expect God to provide the miracle. It will take some heavy lifting, and it will probably tug on your soul in painful ways. At times, your mind might still be a traitor to what your soul knows to be true. But show up anyway. Show up in faith.

By faith, face your Mt. Carmel because it's your calling. By faith, pick up those rocks and start stacking your altar. Do what's yours to do, and allow God to fill in the gaps. By faith, remember He has a plan to prosper and not to harm your children (Jer. 29:11). By faith, trust God has already written each of their stories, knows all of the chapters that come before, during, and after homeschooling, and will use it all for His glory. By faith, do it all afraid, knowing it's only in obedience you'll ever find bravery.

Don't let fear have the final say in your homeschool. Don't just check the "other" box. Check it with bravery! God promised to finish the good work He started in you and your kids. Will you have the audacity to take Him at His Word?

Appendix A

Questions to Ask Before You Start Homeschooling

If you haven't yet pulled the trigger on homeschooling and are inching forward with shaky legs, not knowing if this is really the choice for you and yours, I suggest you begin to seek the biblical advice and wisdom of those God has placed in your spiritual community. It's not by accident He's surrounded you with these people at this moment. Please don't misunderstand me. I'm not saying that human opinion should ever be the scaffolding that holds up your calling. Any human-made support beam will eventually crumble if not braced against the bedrock of Scripture. But much can be gained through the rearview wisdom of Christians who are further on the journey.

By seeking the biblical advice and direction of the spiritual mentors and leaders God has placed in your life, you will gain the kind of safety that only comes with good counsel. Begin to gather the wisdom of Christian family members, pastors, church leaders, and friends whose opinions and values lean firmly on the Word of God. Ask newbies, ask veterans, ask everyone in between.

Obviously, the thoughts of someone who has graduated a child will be different from those whose kids are still in the thick of it, but both perspectives have value. Ask questions, gather answers, and then chew on them a bit. Discuss them with your spouse, stack them against the words of *rhema* God has already given you, and then be willing to sift out opinions that seem too extreme.

Here are a few questions you can ask to help get the meaty answers you're going to need.

What made you initially begin leaning toward your particular schooling choice? What was it about the other options that turned you off?

What are the major pros and cons of your school choice?

What do you think are the biggest pros and cons of the schooling options you didn't choose?

What would you say are the spiritual, emotional, physical, and social dangers of the option you chose?

What were your goals for education? Did your choice meet those goals?

How has your decision affected your overall family time together?

How does your schooling choice help your child stand strong in his faith in our decaying culture?

Did you or do you plan to educate your child in the same way all the way through his high school years? Why or why not?

Did your schooling choice prepare your child academically? Was he ready for college or vocational training?

What is your daily involvement in your child's education?

Were there particular verses in Scripture that helped point you toward one schooling option over another?

Did you switch educational paths midstream, and if so, why? Do you regret your decision? Do you wish you had done it sooner?

Has your child ever asked to be schooled in a different way?

What are your child's most influential social circles? How active are you able to be in these circles?

If you send your child to public school, how do you instill a biblical worldview in him to counter the secular philosophies taught in the school system? Has your child ever been given an assignment in direct opposition to your faith? If so, how did you handle it?

If you homeschool, does your child ever participate in extracurricular activities offered through the school system? If so, how would you rate that experience?

The school debate has a way of bringing out some hard and fast opinions. While personal experiences are good and often helpful, just remember to give each person's answer its proper place. Always park human opinions, no matter how well-intentioned, behind that of God's. Return to those verses of *rhema,* knowing God's counsel should always be the starting point and the finish line of every road you take.

Appendix B

Books for Further Reading

Twentieth-century British educator Charlotte Mason wrote that education is an atmosphere, discipline, and life.[1] As with any vocational calling, to homeschool well, you need to engross yourself in it, continually learning, honing your craft, and gathering the necessary tools to help you build a sturdy foundation. Here are the resources I continue to use for encouragement and equipment.

102 Top Picks for Homeschool Curriculum
by Cathy Duffy (Grove Publishing, 2015)

Packed with simple evaluation grids, goal-setting charts, and extensive reviews of the top homeschooling curriculums on the market, this book provides practical tools to help the new homeschool mom select resources that will fit the particular learning styles of each of her children.

Educating the WholeHearted Child
by Clay and Sally Clarkson (Apologia, 2011)

Now in its third edition, this manual has been guiding parents into the fray since 1994. It is an exhaustive look at biblical homeschooling and is filled with statistics, personal stories, quotations, and helpful book lists all formatted for quick reference.

For the Children's Sake:
Foundations of Education for Home and School
by Susan Schaeffer Macaulay (Crossway, 2009)

Based on the time-tested educational philosophies of Charlotte Mason, this book provides inspiration for the mom seeking to create a culture of lifelong learning in her home. While it addresses the physical needs of a learner, it primarily focuses on emotional and spiritual needs.

Give Your Child the World:
Raising Globally Minded Kids One Book at a Time
by Jamie C. Martin (Zondervan, 2016)

In simplest terms, this is a book of books. It has been organized by continent and reading level in order to provide a mother with a masterfully curated, multicultural reading list for her kids to help them develop knowledge of and compassion for others around the world.

Help! I'm Married to a Homeschooling Mom
by Todd E. Wilson (Moody, 2004)

Popular speaker and humorist Todd Wilson has compiled his best man-to-man wisdom for the homeschooling husband who seeks to better support and meet the practical, everyday needs of his wife.

Homeschooling Gifted Kids
by Cindy West (Our Journey Westward, 2018)

The thought of homeschooling a gifted or advanced learner can feel daunting to the average parent. But it doesn't have to be. This book shows how special considerations can be made in curriculum choices, teaching styles, and long-term plans to make homeschooling the right choice for an accelerated student.

Honey for a Child's Heart
by Gladys Hunt (Zondervan, 2002)

Now in its fourth edition, this annotated book list is a go-to reading companion for any Christian homeschool mom. It's filled with thoughts on how to properly select books for children as well as an updated recommended reading list for tots to teens.

Mere Motherhood: Morning Times, Nursery Rhymes, and My Journey Toward Sanctification
by Cindy Rollins (Circe Institute, 2016)

Part memoir, part mantra—this book is the voice of homeschooling veteran and creator of the Morning Time practice, Cindy Rollins, as she looks back on her home education journey. She candidly shares how she stumbled into homeschooling, how she kept going even when she wanted to give up, and how God used those years with her children in her personal sanctification. It's a bird's-eye view of one mother's real and raw journey.

Project-Based Homeschooling: Mentoring Self-Directed Learners
by Lori McWilliam Pickert (CreateSpace, 2012)

Currently the authoritative guide to strewing or delight-directed learning, this book lays a framework for a mother to encourage self-direction in her homeschool day and provides sound advice for cultivating passions and tapping into a child's natural curiosity.

Ultimate Guide to Homeschooling
by Debra Bell (Apologia, 2009)

Packed with book lists, curriculum suggestions, evaluation tools, and mom-tested tips and solutions, this is a quick-start manual to homeschooling. While it can be read cover-to-cover, it's best used as a reference text for troubleshooting, as it walks a mom through the entire process of setting up and organizing her homeschool.

Acknowledgments

This book might have one name on the cover, but it was certainly not a solo project. I will be forever indebted to an incredible circle of people who linked arms with me every step of the way.

The Unlikely Homeschool community, for the past six years, you have generously given me a peek at both your struggles and strengths. Thank you so much for your candidness. Your bravery in sharing your stories and facing your fears will, no doubt, give other moms the courage to do the same.

Grace, Jas, Brittany, Tiffany, and Rebecca, thank you for being my personal little think tank. Your feedback was indispensable and has helped to shape every thought written here.

Jamie Martin, Kendra Fletcher, Cindy Rollins, Pam Barnhill, Mystie Winkler, Sonya Shafer, Andrew Pudewa, Kristi Clover, Christopher Perrin, Linda Lacour Hobar, Cindy West, Karen DeBeus, and Sarita Holzmann, and it is an honor to be co-laborers with you in the homeschooling community. Thank you for lending your wisdom. This book is so much richer for your words.

Keely Boeving, my agent, thank you for seeing something in this idea from the very beginning and for reminding me of the potential whenever I forgot. Your commitment and hard work on the front end was not missed and can't be appreciated enough.

John Hinkley, Ashley Torres, and the team at Moody Publishers, thank you so much for valuing the needs of homeschooling mothers and for allowing me to give a voice to their fears. Your devotion to biblical accuracy and to the unity of believers is unparalleled.

Annette LaPlaca, it was not by accident that out of all the editors in the world, I was gifted with one who has spent years homeschooling her children. Only a kind God could have orchestrated such an alliance. Thank you for not only seeing my words but also my heart on the page.

Psalm 68:6 says that "God sets the lonely in families" (NIV). Beth, God knew I was lonely for a writing family, and He sent me you. You will never know how your outstretched arms came at just the right time. Thank you for loving hard on words and for letting me do the same.

Emily and Jacqui, I'm so glad I don't have to hide all my secrets with you. I count our shared friendship as one of the miracles of my life. You are my sweatpants in a sea of skinny jeans, my comfort food. Thank you for cheering me on every step of the way as I wrote and for dragging me when necessary.

Sarah, you may not even remember, but three years ago, you handed me direction. When I began tossing around thoughts for a book, you encouraged me to write what I knew. "Tell them the same thing that you're always telling me: You can do it! Remind them about God's plan for their homeschool," you said. I hope I have. And to Veronica and Sheri, my other two sisters and second mothers, you have been my life-long encouragers and protectors. This year has been no exception.

Glen and Maureen, your homeschooling legacy is written on every page of this book. You had the courage to do it first. Thank you for passing the torch. You've shown me how to carry it well.

Mom, thank you for not just loving me all of my days, but also for liking me. You've over-supported and over-valued everything I've ever done, including this book. You've heard every word twice. You've cried and clapped at all the right places. If I can champion my children half as well as you've always championed me, I know they'll walk tall into adulthood. Paul, your continued prayer support has upheld me from the moment I put the first letter on the page. Dad, my love for words was birthed all those years ago when you took me on library dates. Consider this book my belated but sincerest "Thank you."

Madeline, Reese, Finnlae, Jack, and Jude, thank you for joining me in this grand experiment called homeschooling. Your births made me a mother, and now your stories have made me an author. In every way, you are my dreams wrapped in skin. It is my greatest joy to call you mine.

Dain, thank you for putting up with my elaborate hustle and controlled chaos these past six years of blogging, speaking, and writing. You know all my ugliness and yet you stick around anyway. Thank you for believing in this book even when I was too scared to and for pushing me toward the bravery that was mine all along in Christ. Next to Him, you're my most favorite.

Jesus, thank you for seeing past all my messy imperfections and for loving me perfectly. You have given me a place to belong where I am completely allowed to be me, no strings attached. You are the only reason I can be brave. You are all the reasons.

Notes

Chapter 1: When You Check the Wrong Box

1. Eric J. Isenberg, "The Choice of Public, Private, or Home Schools: Occasional Paper No. 132," National Center for the Study of Privatization in Education, Teachers College, Columbia University, New York, 2006.

2. Jamie Martin, "Are You a Good Enough Teacher?," Simple Homeschool, August 15, 2011, https://simplehomeschool.net/are-you-a-good-enough-teacher/.

Chapter 2: Calling or Coincidence

1. Kendra Fletcher, personal interview, quoted with permission.

2. Clay Clarkson and Sally Clarkson, *Educating the WholeHearted Child* (Anderson: Apologia Press, 2011), 13.

Chapter 3: The Path to Bravery

1. Holley Gerth, *You're Made for a God-Sized Dream* (Grand Rapids: Revell, 2013), 102.

2. Cindy Rollins, personal interview, quoted with permission.

Chapter 4: Watch Your Own Dice

1. Pam Barnhill, personal interview, quoted with permission.

2. Melanie Lindner, "What People Are Still Willing to Pay For," *Forbes*, January 1, 2009, https://www.forbes.com/2009/01/15/self-help-industry-ent-sales-cx_ml_0115selfhelp.html.

Chapter 5: When You Have One of *Those* Kids

1. Saad Shaikh, M.D., and James Leonard-Amedeo, "The Deviating Eyes of Michelangelo's David," *Journal of the Royal Society of Medicine*, February 2005, https://www.ncbi.nlm.nih.gov/pmc/articles/PMC1079389/.

2. Mystie Winckler, "Why You Want to Give Up Homeschooling," Simply Convivial, February 3, 2015, www.simplyconvivial.com/2015/why-you-want-to-give-up-homeschooling/.

Chapter 6: Struggling to Teach a Struggler

1. Sonya Shafer, personal interview, quoted with permission.

Chapter 7: Little People and Big Messes

1. Andrew Pudewa, "Now Is the Time," Institute for Excellence in Writing, 2009, www.iew.com/schools/help-support/resources/article/now-time.

2. Julie Bogart, personal interview, quoted with permission.

Chapter 8: One Crazy Day Away from Crisis

1. Judy Burris and Wayne Richards, *The Life Cycles of Butterflies* (North Adams, MA: Storey Publishing, 2006), 11.

2. Kristi Clover, personal interview, quoted with permission.

Chapter 9: It's Homeschool, Not School-at-Home

1. Raymond S. Moore and Dorothy N. Moore, *Better Late Than Early: A New Approach to Your Child's Education* (New York: Reader's Digest Press, 1975), 22.

2. Christopher Perrin, personal interview, quoted with permission.

3. Matthew Lieberman, "Education and the Social Brain," *Trends in Neuroscience and Education* 1 (2012): 3–9, http://www.academia.edu/2790088/Trends_in_Neuroscience_and_Education.

4. Charlotte Mason, *An Essay Towards a Philosophy of Education* (New York: Routledge, 2012), 240.

5. John Holt and Pat Faring, *Teach Your Own: The John Holt Book of Homeschooling* (Cambridge: Perseus Publishing, 2003), 279.

Chapter 10: A Guilt-Free Year

1. Linda Lacour Hobar, personal interview, quoted with permission.

2. See Jamie C. Martin, "To the Mama Who Feels Like She's Not Getting Enough Done (My Productivity Secret)," Steady Mom, April 22, 2015, http://www.steadymom.com/2015/04/to-the-mom-who-feels-like-she-never-gets-enough-done.html.

3. Margaret L. Kern and Howard S. Friedman, "Early Educational Milestones as Predictors of Lifelong Academic Achievement, Midlife Adjustment, and Longevity," *Journal of Applied Developmental Psychology* 30, no. 4 (2008): 419–30.

4. Ibid.

5. Fred Rogers, Goodreads.com, https://www.goodreads.com/quotes/885196-play-is-often-talked-about-as-if-it-were-a.

6. Aristotle, BrainyQuote, www.brainyquote.com/quotes/aristotle_408592.

Chapter 11: Your Spot on the Wall

1. Christopher Perrin, personal interview, quoted with permission.

2. R.W. Ward, *Commentary on 1 & 2 Timothy and Titus* (Waco, TX: Word, 1974), 171.

3. G. K. Chesterton, Goodreads.com, https://www.goodreads.com/quotes/119556-a-dead-thing-can-go-with-the-stream-but-only.

4. Saint Augustine, *The Confessions of Saint Augustine*, trans. Edward B. Pusey (Digireads.com Publishing, 2016), 13.

Chapter 12: The End in Mind

1. Sir Henry Newbolt, "The Building of the Temple," PoemHunter.com, https://www.poemhunter.com/poem/the-building-of-the-temple/.

2. Charlotte Mason, *Home Education* (Jilliby: Living Book Press, 2017), 118.

3. Elisabeth Elliot, Goodreads.com, https://www.goodreads.com/quotes/915294-don-t-dig-up-in-doubt-what-you-planted-in-faith.

4. Pam Barnhill, personal interview, quoted with permission.

Chapter 13: Check the Box with Bravery

1. Cindy West, personal interview, quoted with permission.
2. Max Lucado, Goodreads.com, https://www.goodreads.com/quotes/266195-feed-your-fears-and-your-faith-will-starve-feed-your.

Appendix B: Books for Further Reading

1. Charlotte Mason, *Parents and Children* (Jilliby, New South Wales: Living Book Press, 2017), 247.

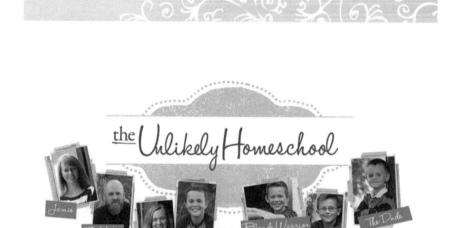

Find out more from Jamie Erickson at:

WWW.THEUNLIKELYHOMESCHOOL.COM

FROM EDUCATIONAL AND PARENTING EXPERT DR. KATHY KOCH

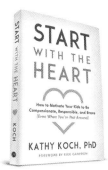

Dr. Kathy Koch will teach you proven strategies that move your child from, "I can't, I won't," to "I can, I will, and I did." We can do better than behavior modification. We can change our children's hearts and teach them to be motivated toward godly and good goals.

978-0-8024-1885-2

Screens and Teens applauds the good aspects of the digital age, but also alerts parents to how technology contributes to self-centered character, negative behaviors, and beliefs that inhibit spiritual growth, prescribing manageable solutions regardless of the level of their teen's involvement.

978-0-8024-1269-0

Do you wish your child could see how smart he or she is? Find hope in *8 Great Smarts*! You'll be equipped and empowered to discover and affirm your child's unique smarts, which can help you motivate more successful learning and guide your child behaviorally, spiritually, and relationally.

978-0-8024-1359-8

**MOODY
Publishers®**

From the Word to Life®

also available as eBooks